Phonics/Phonemic Awareness

Practice Book Kindergarten

Contents

Name_____

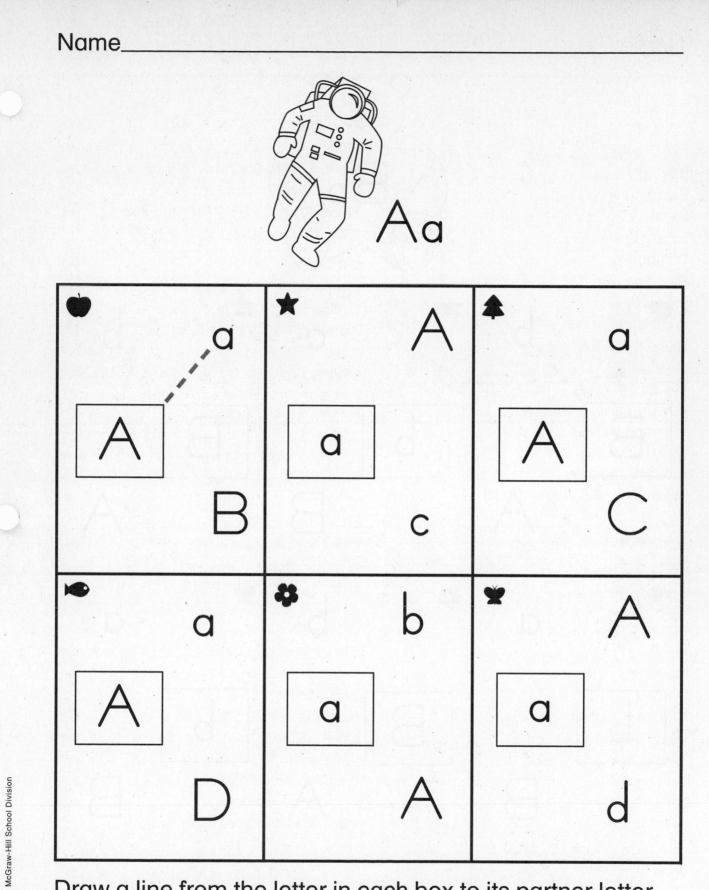

Aa

Draw a line from the letter in each box to its partner letter.

 Grade K

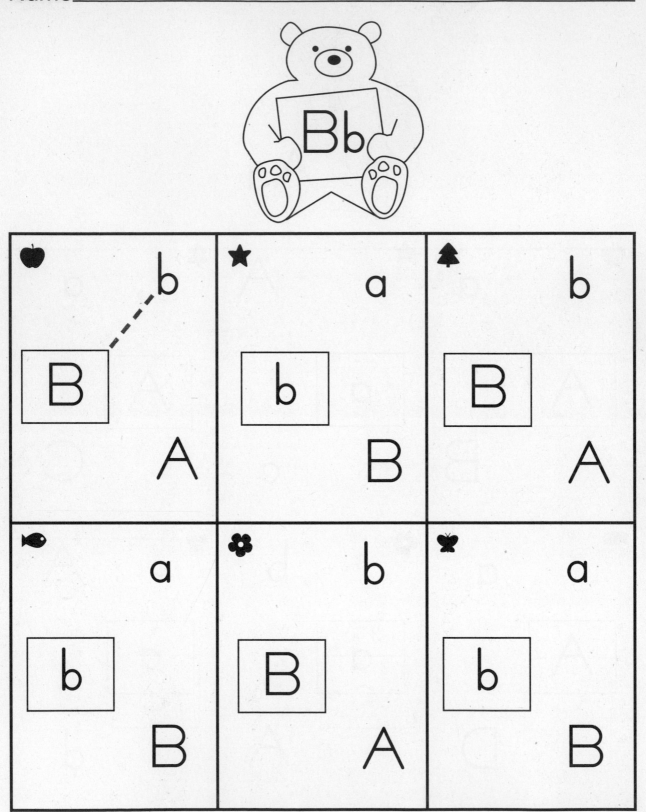

Draw a line from the letter in the box to its partner letter.

Name_____

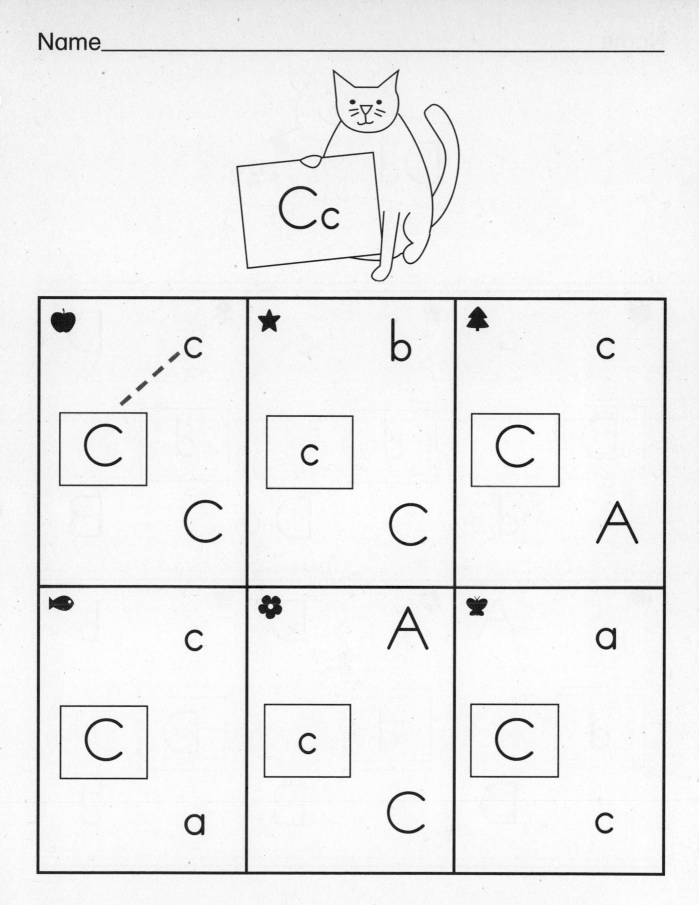

Draw a line from the letter in the box to its partner letter.

Dd

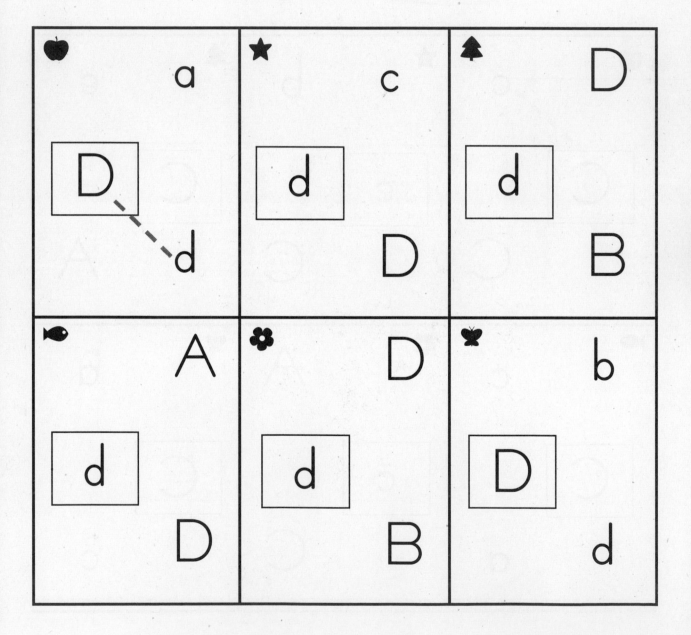

a

D····d

c

d

D

D

d

B

A

d

D

D

d

B

b

D

d

Draw a line from the letter in the box to its partner letter.

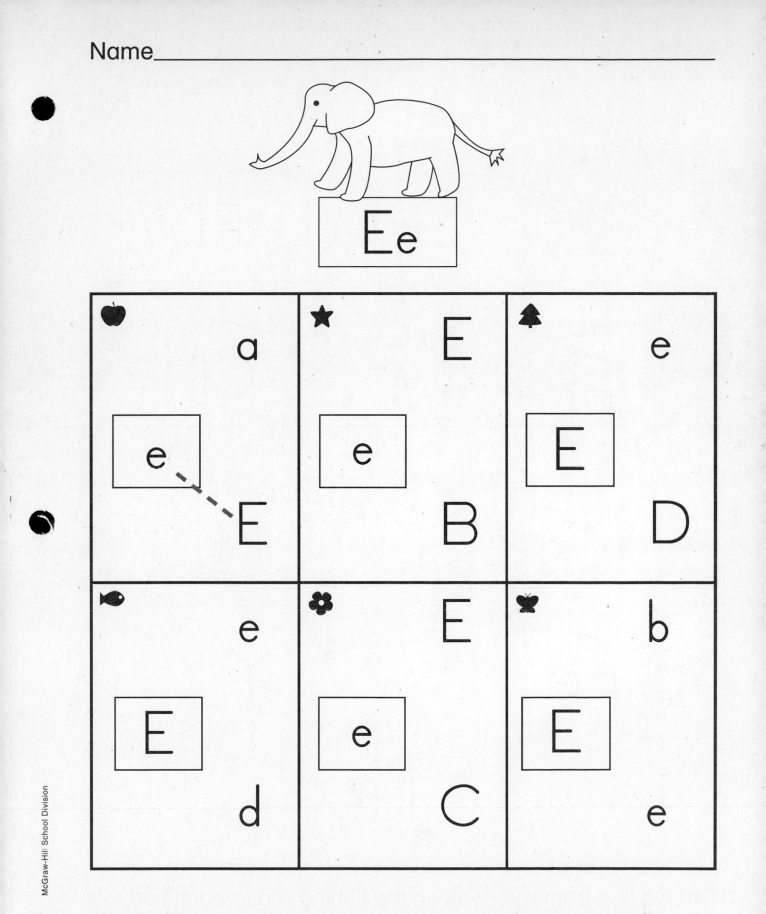

Draw a line from the letter in the box to its partner letter.

Name_____

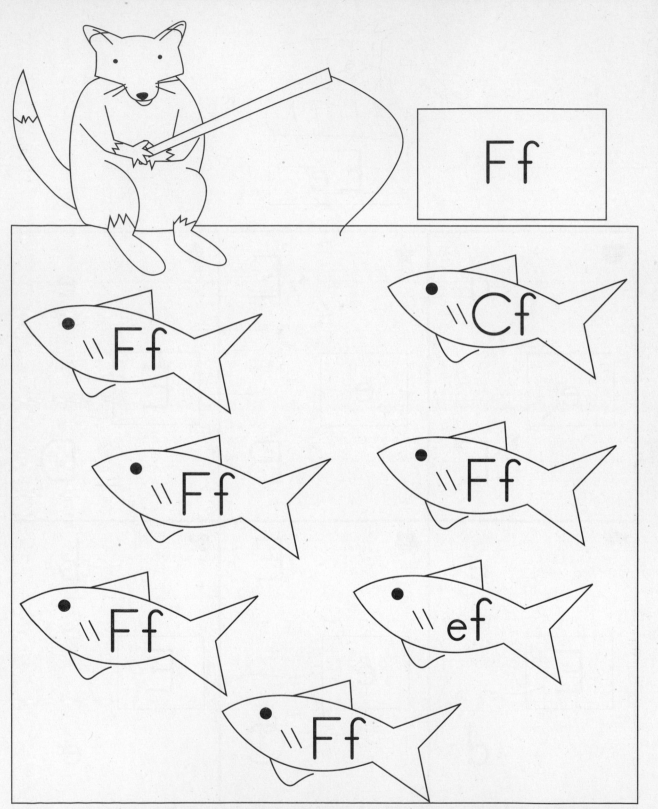

Ff

Ff

Cf

Ff

Ff

Ff

ef

Ff

Draw a line from the hook on the fishing rod to each fish that has the partner letters *Ff.*

Name_____

Color each goat that has the partner letters *Gg* on it.

Name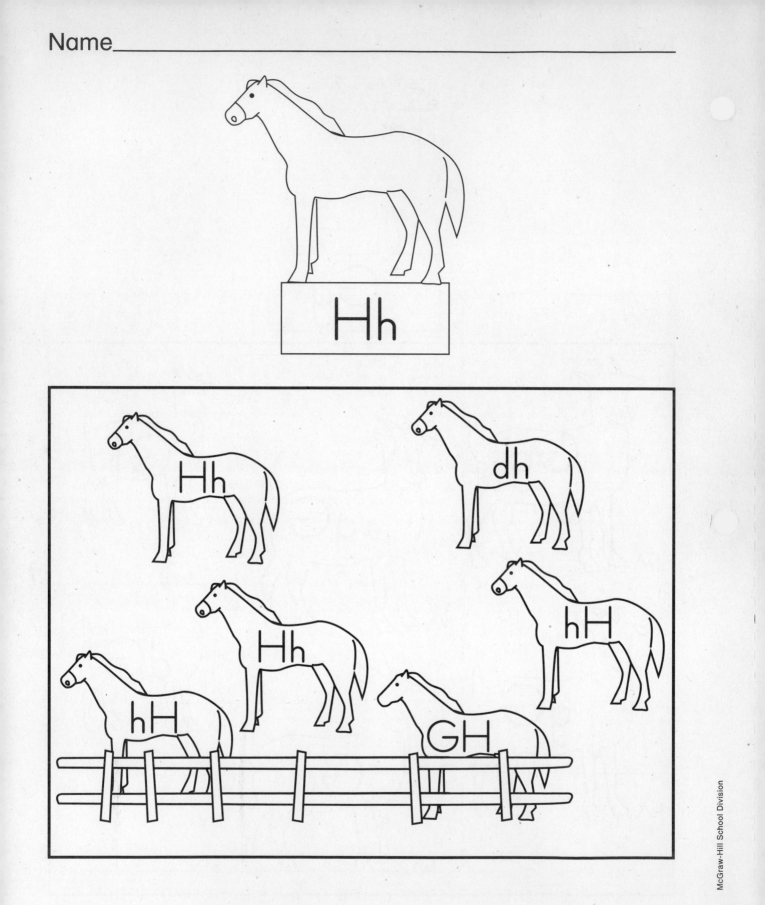

Color each horse that has the partner letters *Hh* on it.

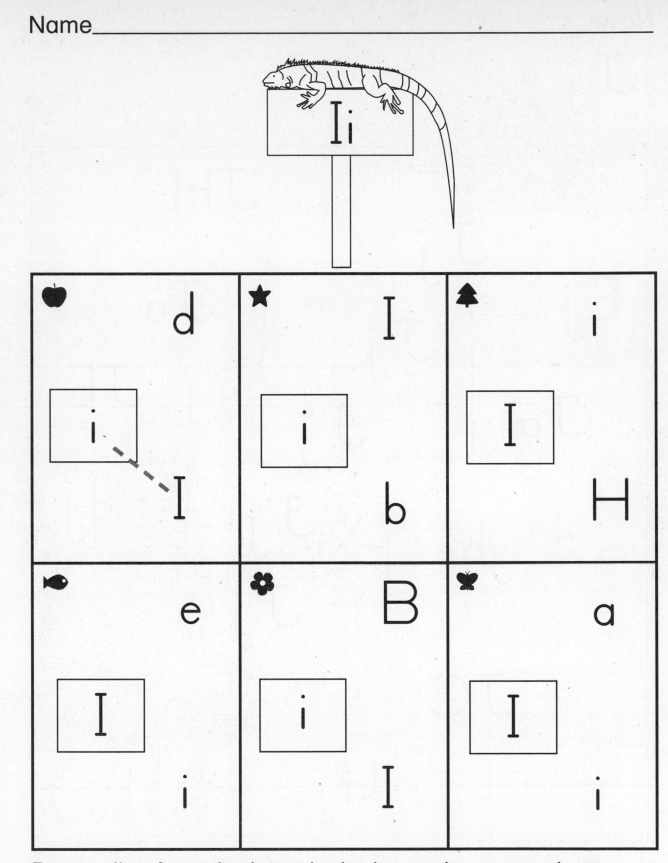

Draw a line from the letter in the box to its partner letter.

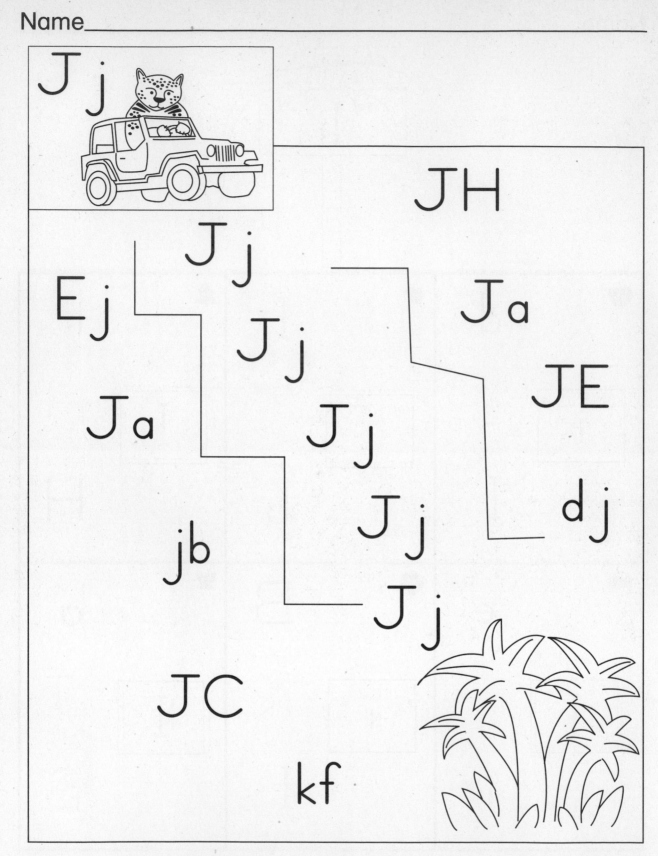

Help the jaguar get to the jungle. Draw a line on the path with the partner letters *Jj*.

Name_____

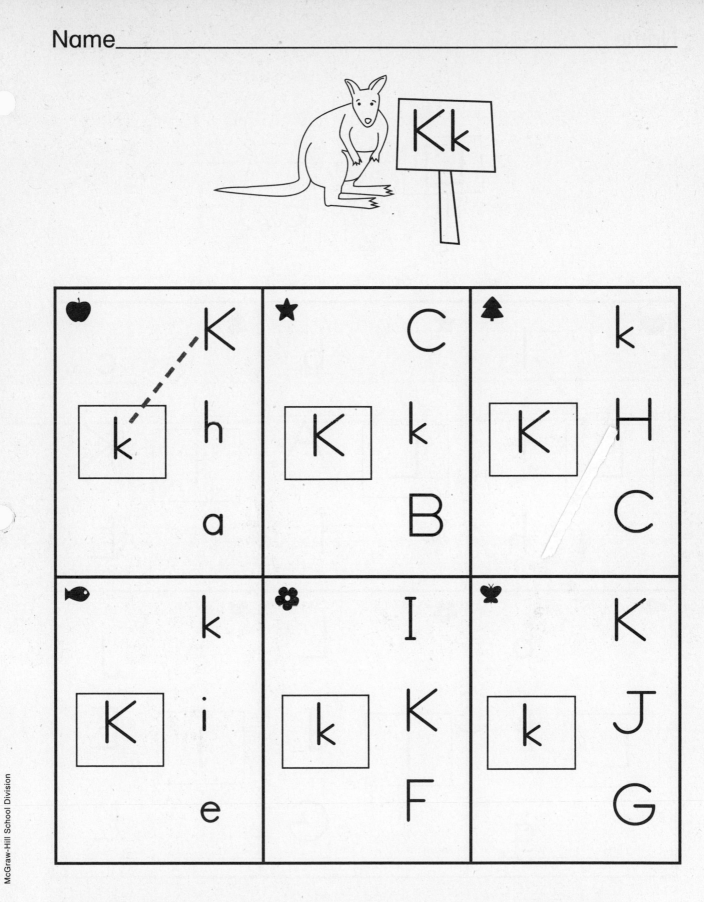

Draw a line from the letter in the box to its partner letter.

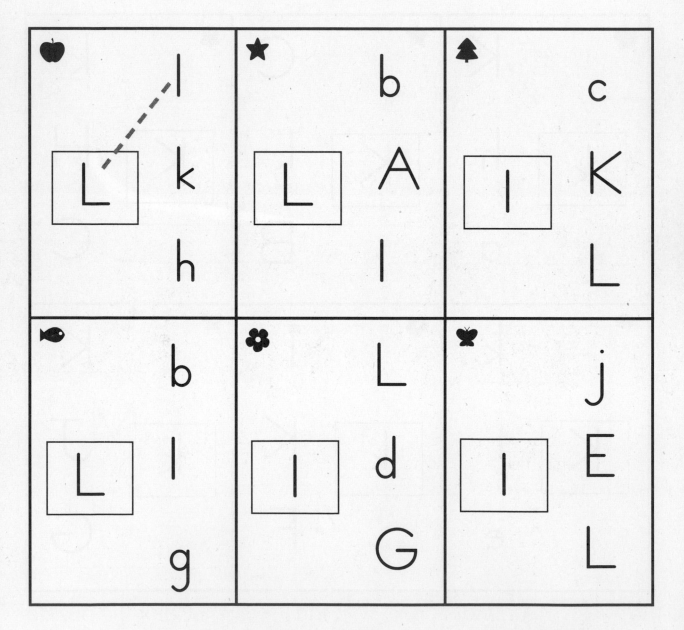

Draw a line from the letter in the box to its partner letter.

Grade K

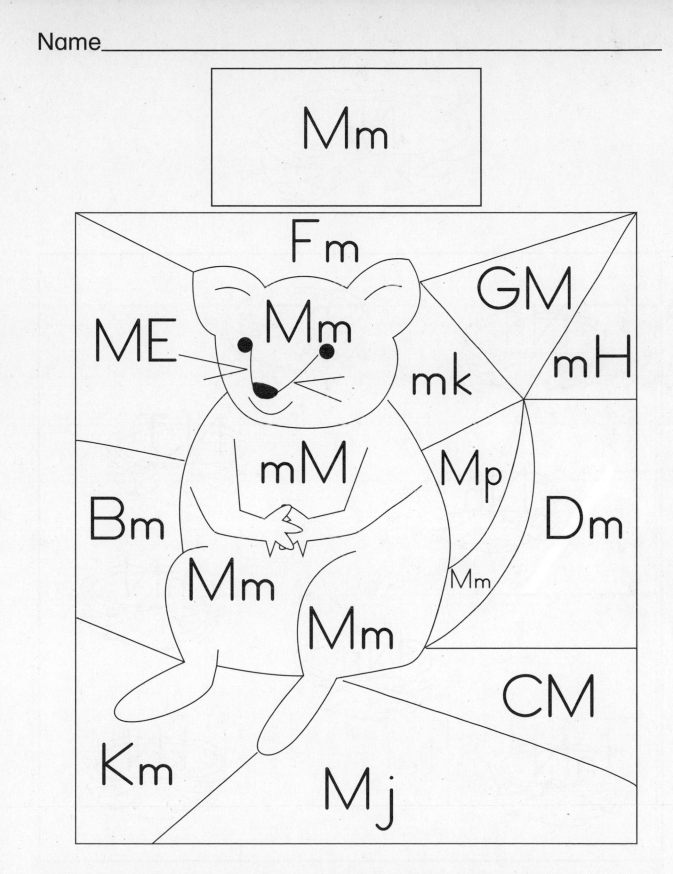

Mm

What small animal begins with the letter *m*? Color the puzzle
pieces with the partner letters *Mm* one color to find out.

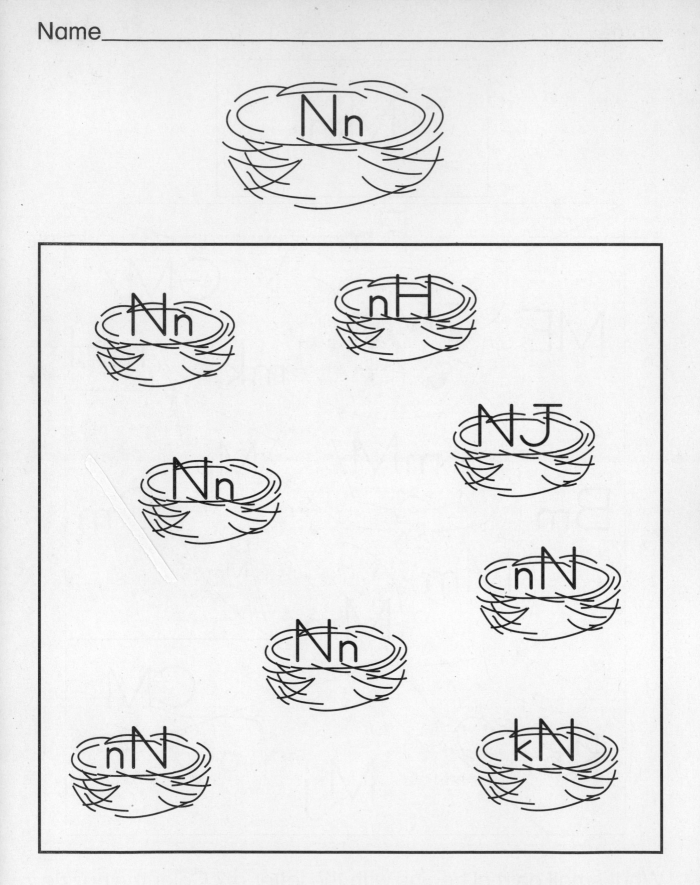

Color each nest that has the partner letters *Nn* in it.

Color each ox that has the partner letters Oo on it.

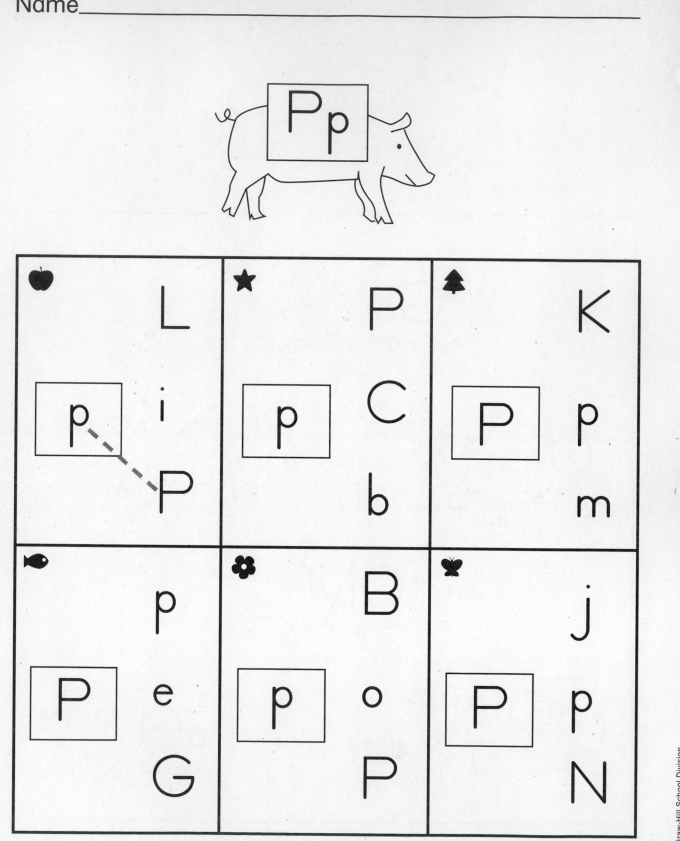

Draw a line from the letter in the box to its partner letter.

Name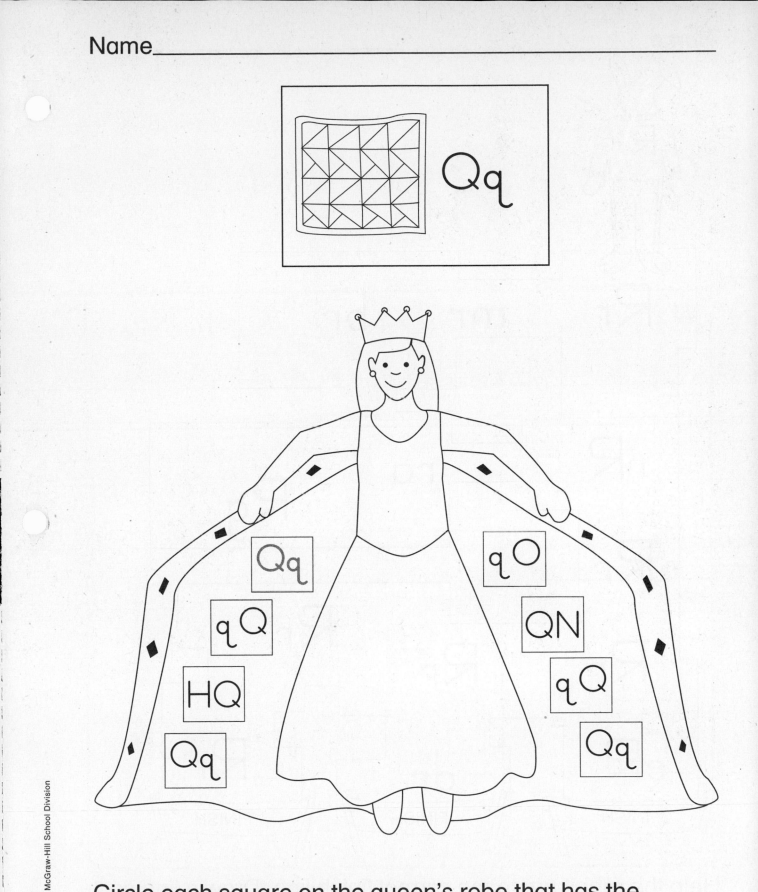

Circle each square on the queen's robe that has the partner letters *Qq* on it.

 8 Grade K

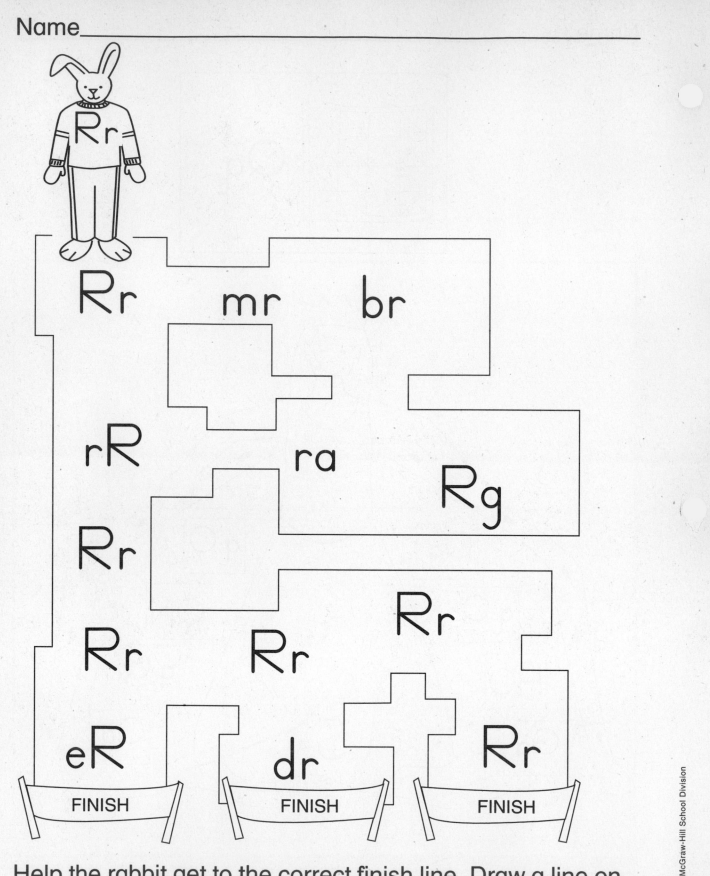

Help the rabbit get to the correct finish line. Draw a line on the path with the partner letters *Rr* to the finish line.

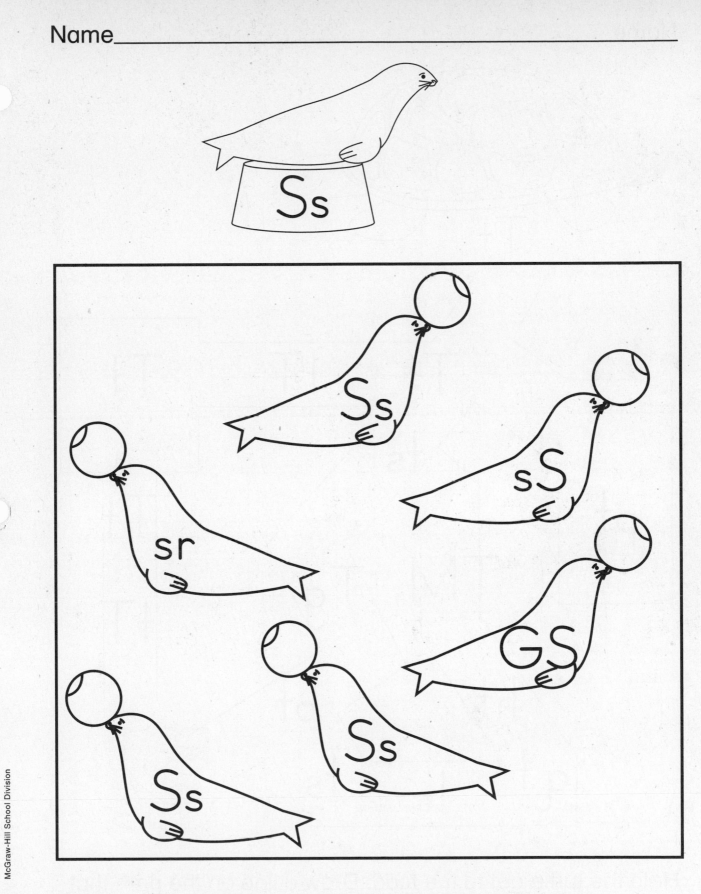

Color each seal that has the partner letters *Ss* on it.

Grade K

Name_____

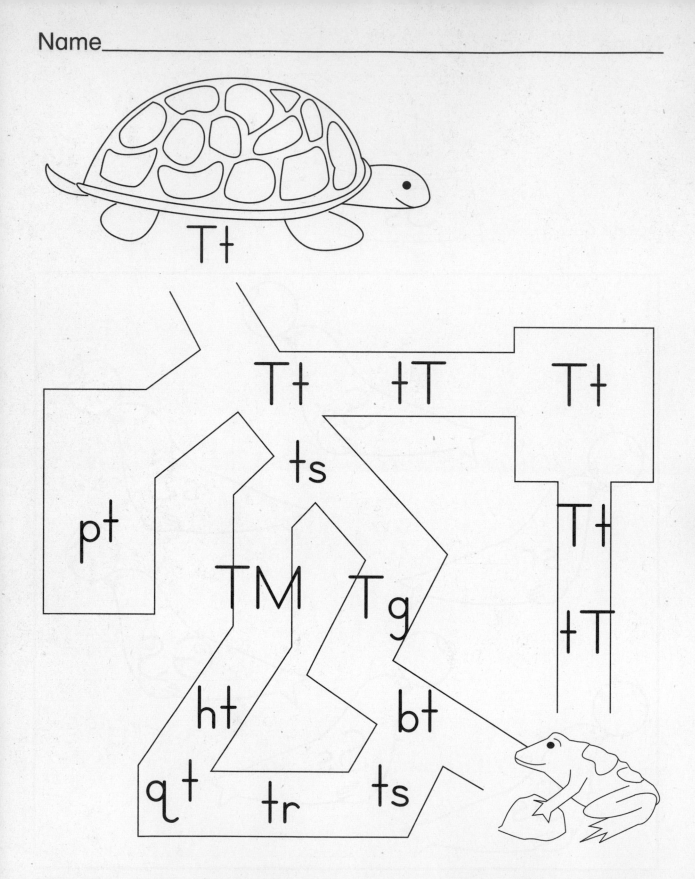

Help the turtle get to the toad. Draw a line on the path that has the partner letters *Tt* on it.

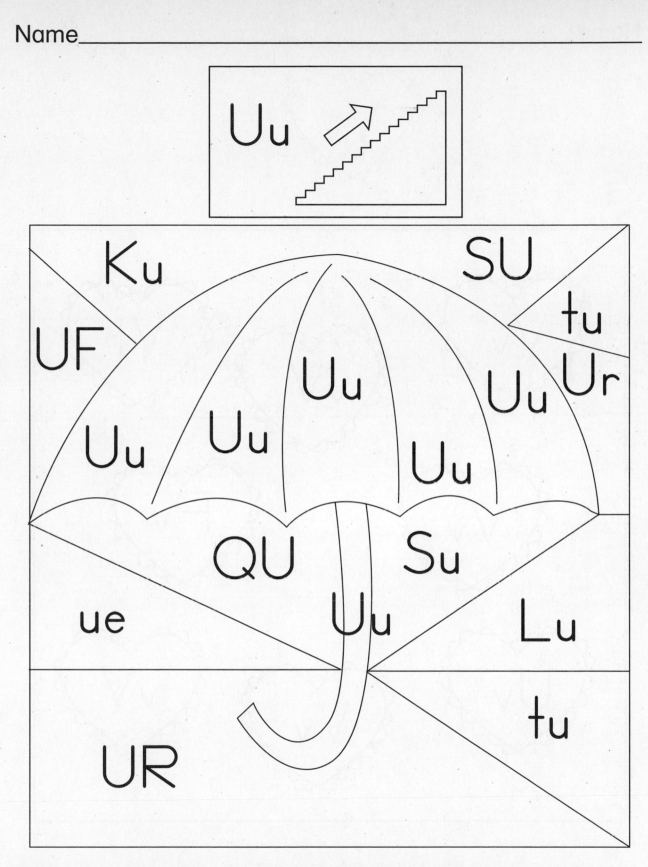

What do you need in the rain? Color all the puzzle pieces with the partner letters *Uu* one color to find out.

Color each valentine with the partner letters *Vv* on it.

Name_____

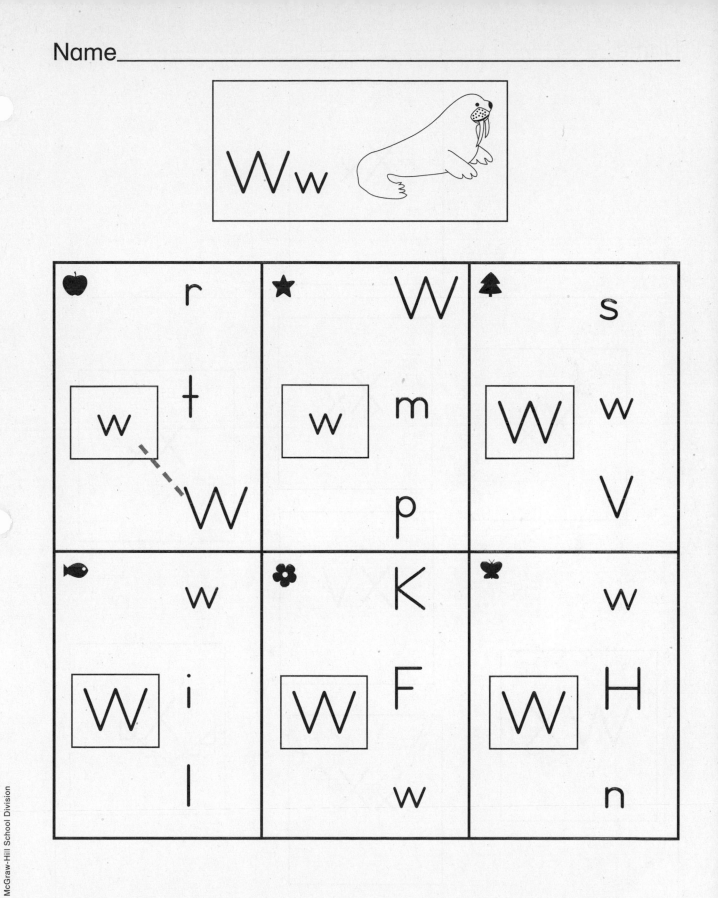

Draw a line from the letter in the box to its partner letter.

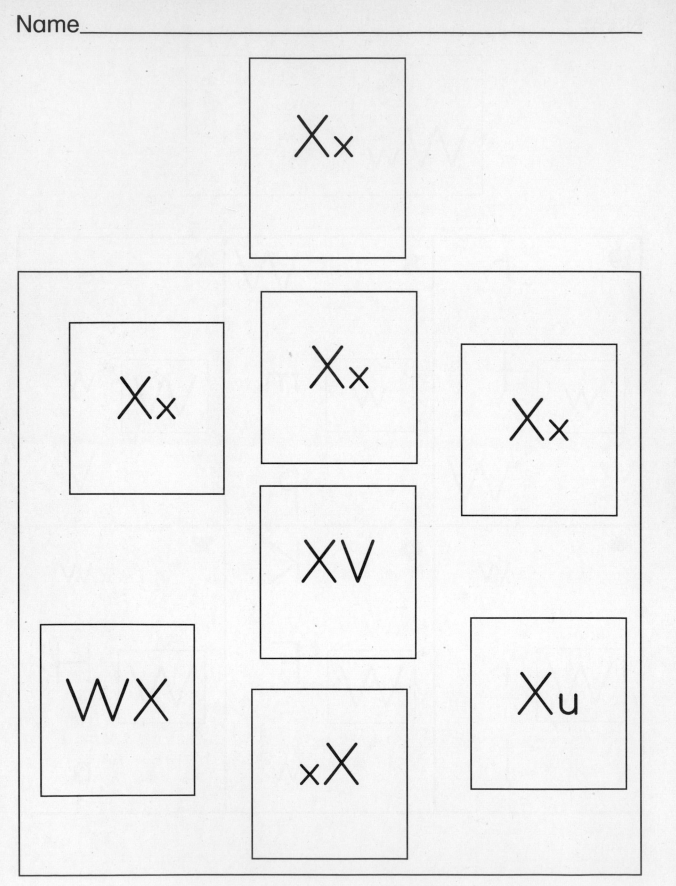

Circle each box that has the partner letters *Xx* in it.

Circle each yak that has the partner letters *Yy* on it.

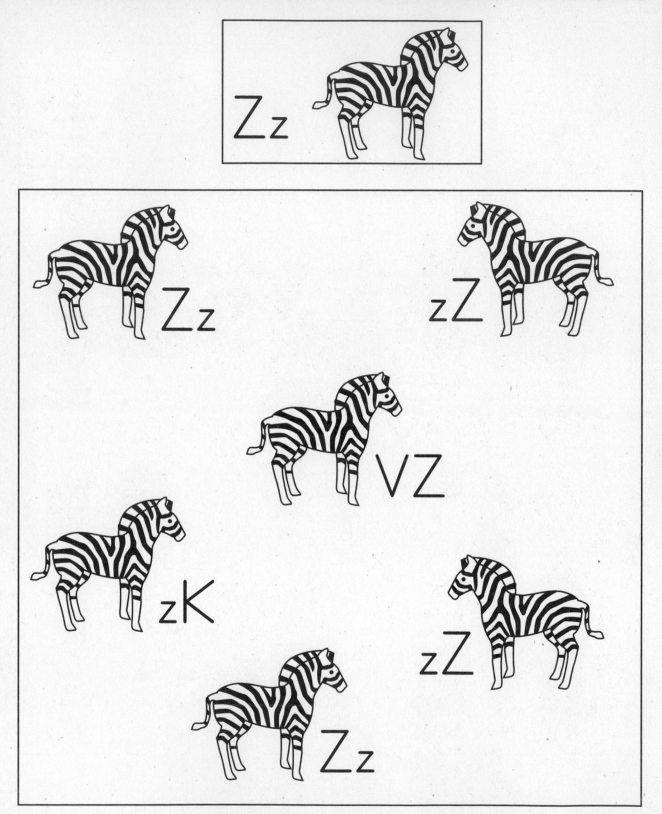

Circle each zebra that has the partner letters Zz next to it.

Say the name of the pictures. Draw a line from each picture whose name begins like *nest* to the picture of the nest.

Say the name of each picture. If the name begins with the same sound as *nest*, write *Nn* on the line.

Name_____

Say the name of the pictures in each box. Circle the picture whose name ends with the same sound as *fan*.

 Grade K

Final /n/ **29**

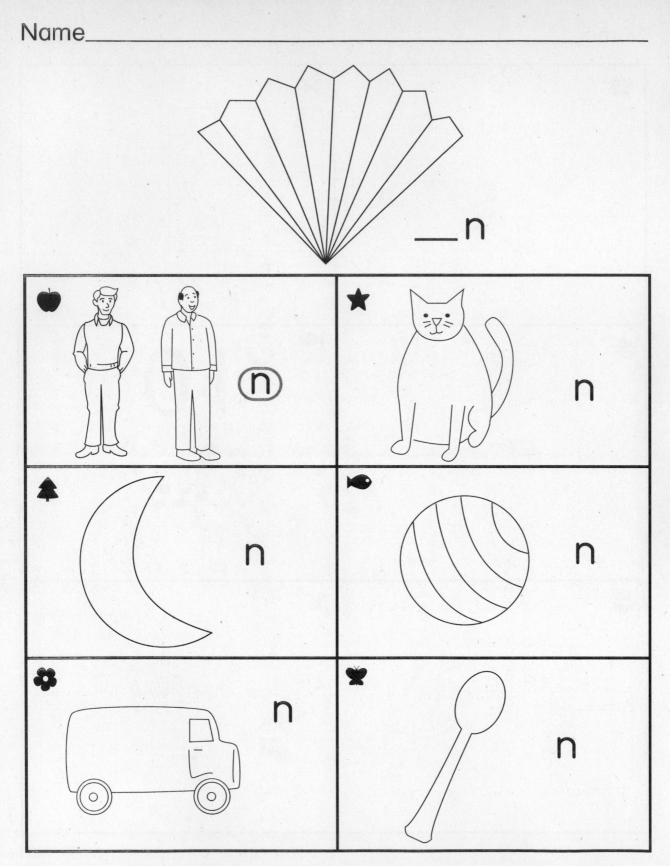

__n

Say the name of each picture. If the picture name ends with the same sound as *fan,* circle the *n.*

N

n

Trace and write *Nn.* Then circle the pictures whose names begin with the same sound as *nest.*

Trace and write *Nn* on the lines.

Name_____

Say the name of the pictures. Draw a line from each picture whose name begins like *apple* to the picture of the apple.

Say the name of each picture. If the name begins with the same sound as *apple*, write *Aa* on the line.

Name_____

Say the name of the pictures. Draw a line from each picture
whose name has the same middle sound as *cat* to the
picture of the cat.

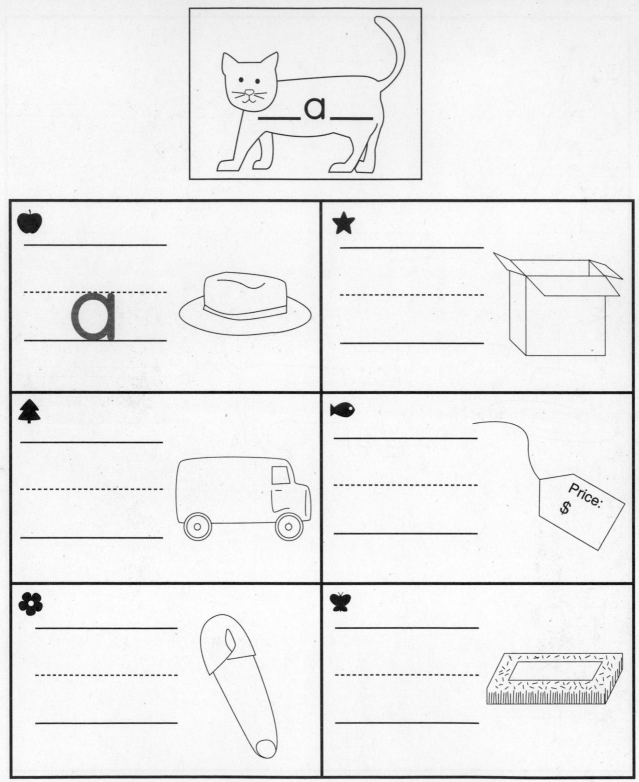

Say the name of each picture. If the name has the same middle sound as *cat,* write *a* on the line.

Name_____

A

a

Trace and write *Aa.* Then circle the pictures whose names begin with the same sound as *apple.*

Name_____

● ★ Trace the letters and read the names.

🌲 ● Write the names on the lines and read the names.

38 Blending with Short *a*

Grade K

4

McGraw-Hill School Division

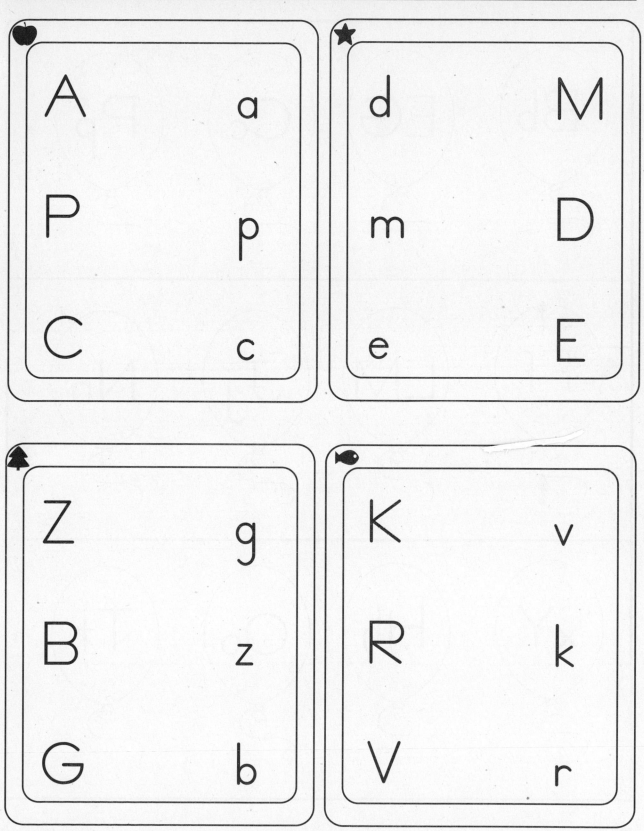

Draw a line to match the partner letters in each chalkboard.

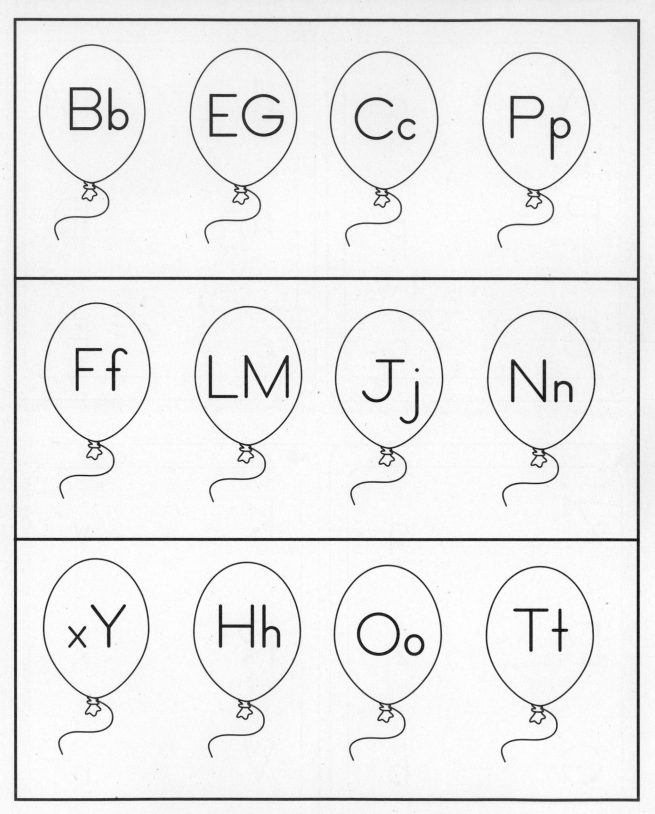

Color each balloon that has partner letters in it.

My

My

My

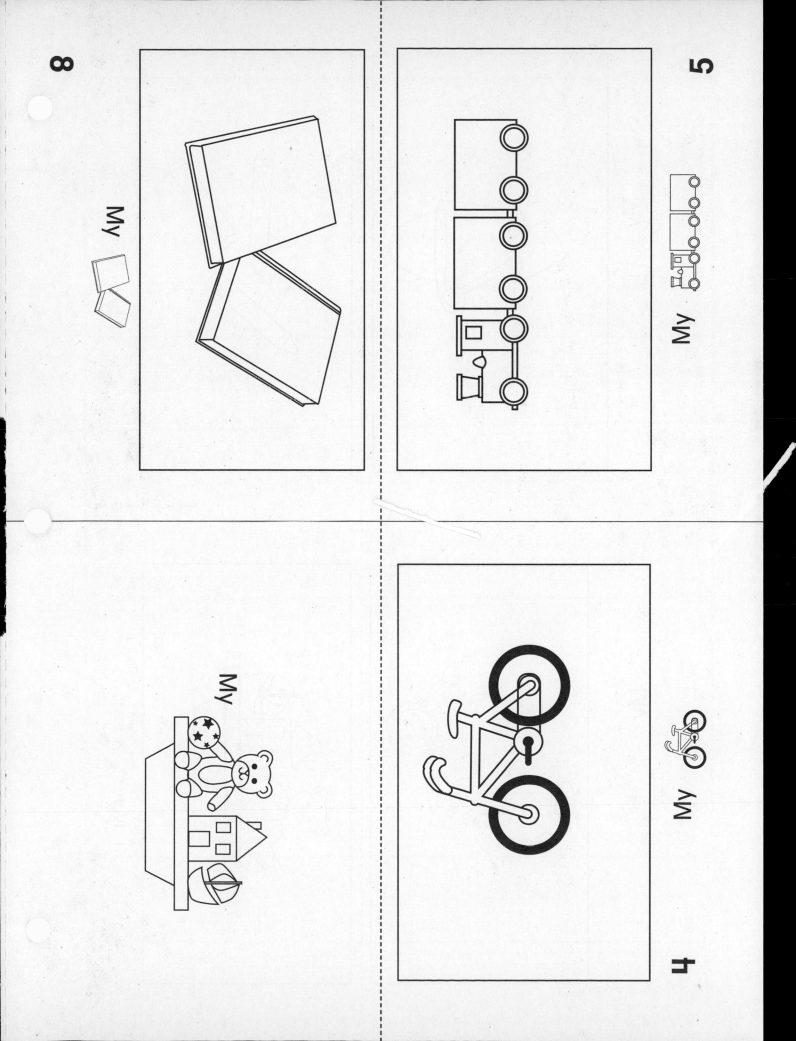

My

My

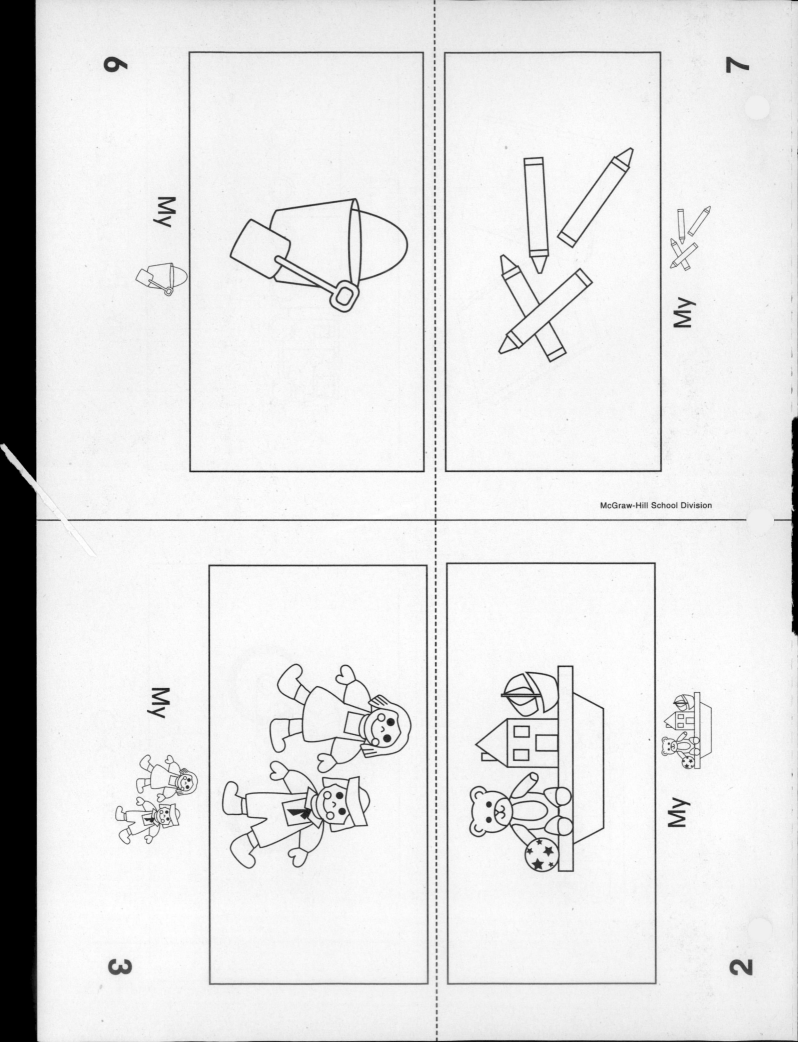

My

My

My

My

Look at the picture. Color the things whose names begin with the same sound as *duck*.

Say the name of each picture. If the name begins with the same sound as *duck*, write *Dd* on the line.

Name_____

Say the name of the pictures in each box. Color the picture whose name ends with the same sound as *bed*.

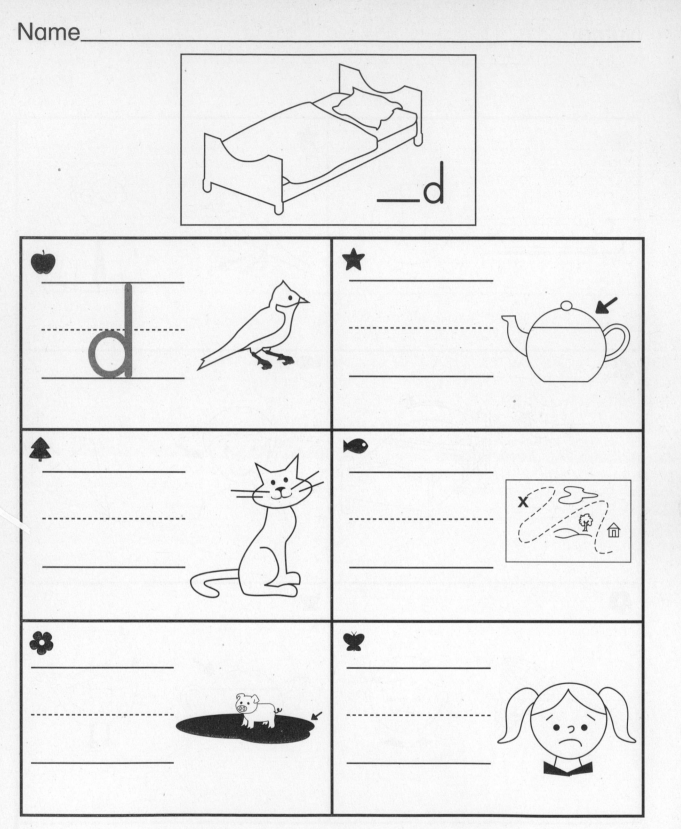

Say the name of each picture. If the picture name ends
with the same sound as *bed*, write *d* on the line.

D

d

Trace and write *Dd.* Circle the pictures whose names begin with the same sound as *duck.*

McGraw-Hill School Division

Grade K

Write the missing letters for the names *Nan* and *Dan*.
Then write the name of each child below their picture.

Say the names of the pictures. Draw a line from the pictures whose names begin like *sock* to the picture of the sock.

Name_____

Write *Ss* on the lines. Then say the names of the pictures.
Color each picture whose name begins like *sock*.

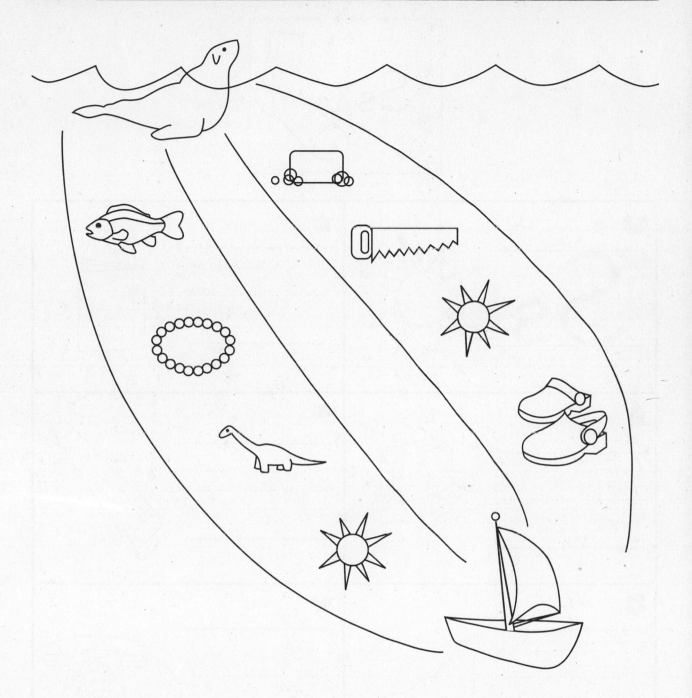

Help the seal get to the toy sailboat. Say the name of each picture. Draw a line on the path that shows only pictures whose names begin with the same sound as *seal*.

Name_____

Say the name of each picture. If the name begins the same as *sock*, write *Ss* on the line.

S

s

Trace and write *Ss*. Then circle the pictures whose names begin with the same sound as *sock*.

Grade K

Name_____

Read the words. Then circle the word that names the picture.

Look at the picture. Color the things whose names begin with the same sound as *moon*.

Grade K

Write *Mm* on the lines. Then say the names of the pictures.
Color each picture whose name begins like *Moon*.

Say the name of the pictures. Draw a line from each picture whose name ends with the same sound as *drum* to the picture of the drum.

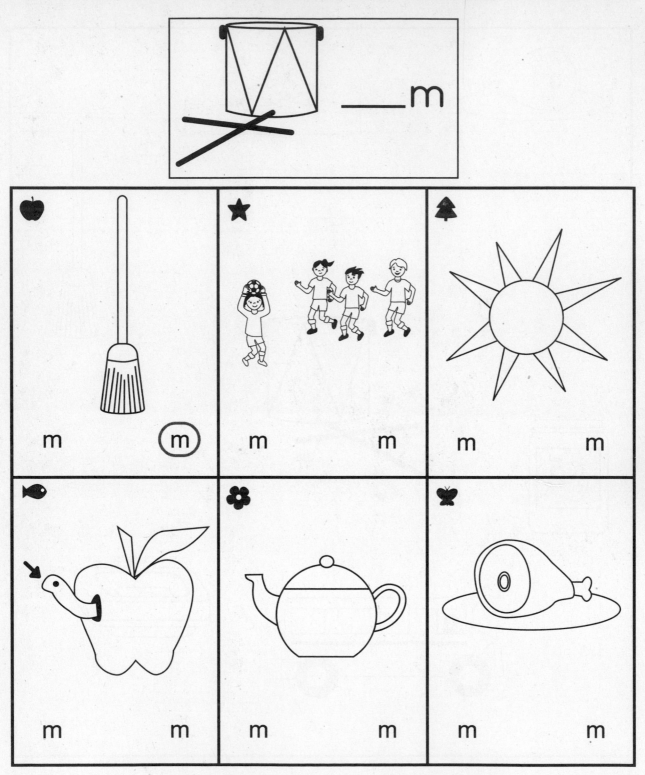

Say the name of each picture. If the picture name ends with the same sound as *drum,* circle the last *m.*

Name_____

M

m

Trace and write *Mm.* Then circle the pictures whose names begin with the same sound as *moon.*

Grade K

Trace the letters. Then read the words.

Name_____

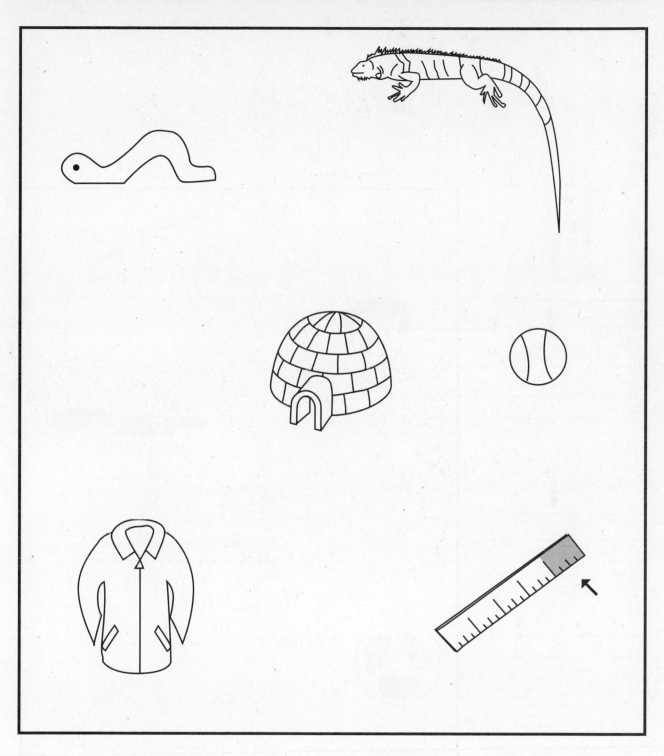

Say the names of the pictures. Draw a line from each picture whose name begins like *igloo* to the igloo.

Write *Ii* on the lines. Then say the names of the pictures.
Circle each picture whose name begins with *Ii*.

Grade K

Say the names of the pictures. Draw a line from each picture whose name has the same middle sound as *pig* to the pig.

Say the name of each picture. If the name has the same middle sound as in *pig*, write *i* on the line.

I

i

Trace and write *Ii*. Then circle the pictures whose names begin with the same sound as *igloo*.

Grade K

Name_____

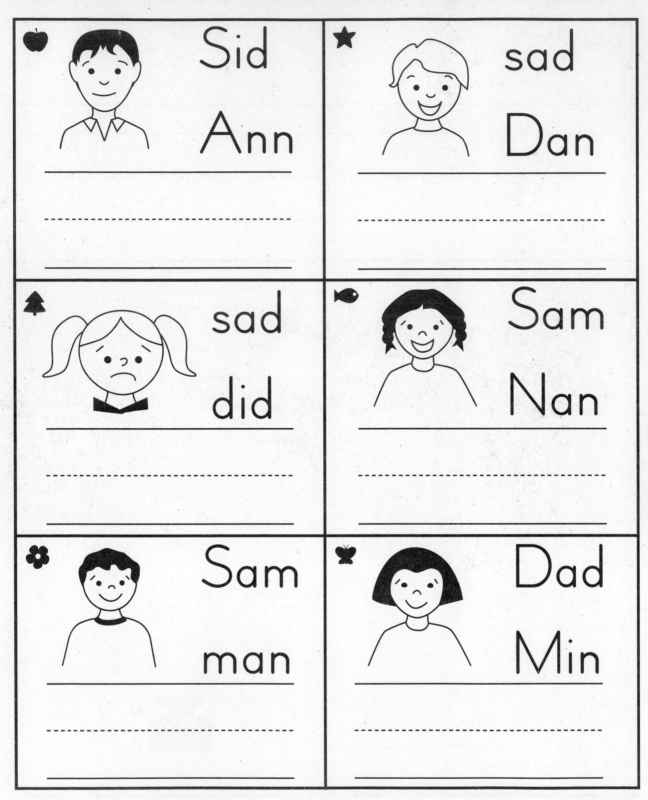

Read the words. Circle the word that names the picture.
Then write the word.

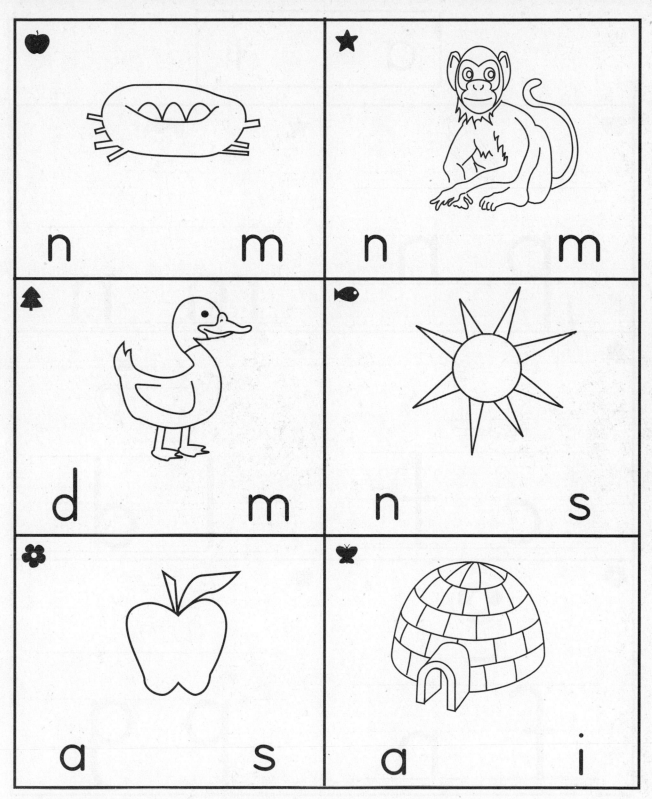

n   m   n   m

d   m   n   s

a   s   a   i

Say each name. Circle the letter that stands for the
beginning sound.

6   Grade K

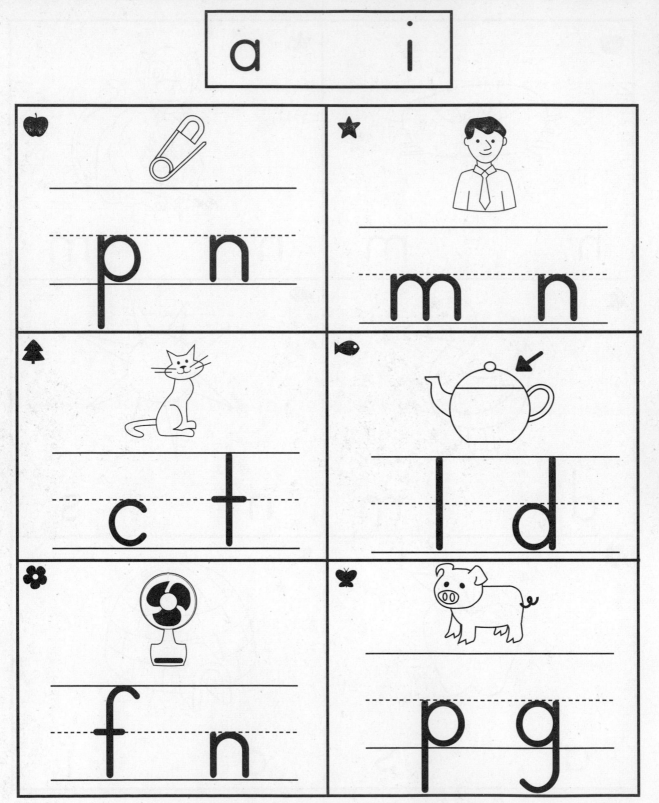

Say each picture name. Choose a letter from the box that stands for the middle sound. Write the letter on the line.

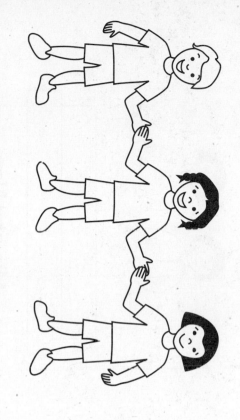

Nan and Min and Dan

Min and Dan

Nan and Min and Dan

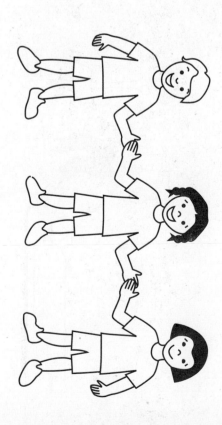

Sid and Dan

Min and Nan

Min and Sam

Sam and Dan

Sid and Sam

7

Name_____

Say each picture name. Circle the pictures in each row whose names begin with the same sound as *turtle.*

Say the name of each picture. If the name begins with the same sound as *turtle,* write *Tt* on the line.

Name_____

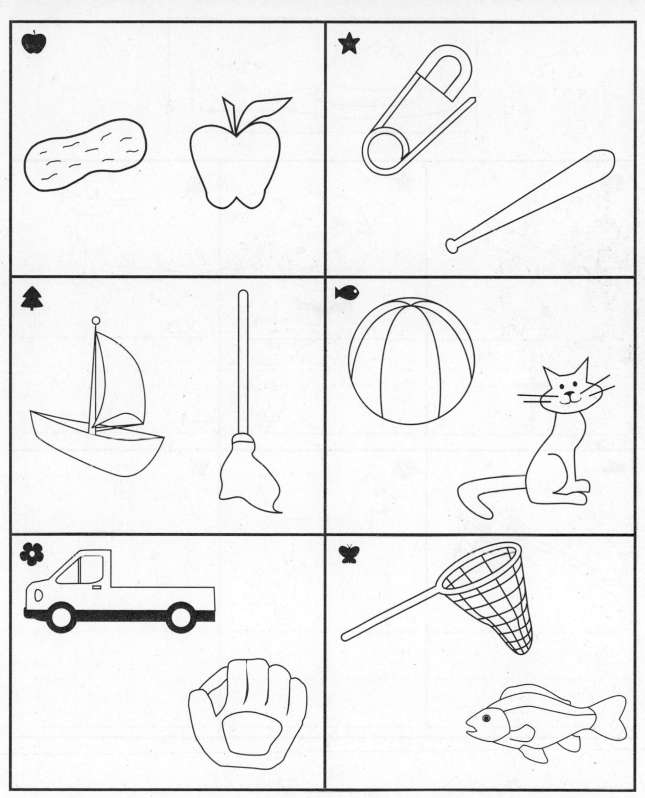

Say the picture names. Circle the pictures whose names end with the same sound as *hat.*

Say the name of each picture. If the picture name ends with the same sound as *hat*, write *t* on the line.

Trace and write *Tt*. Color the pictures whose names begin with the same sound as *turtle*.

8 Grade K

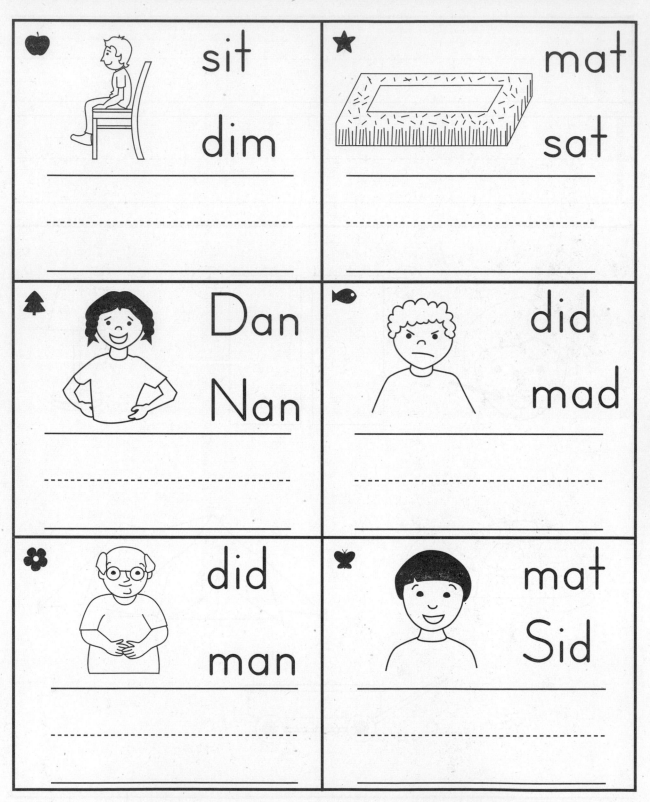

sit
dim

mat
sat

Dan
Nan

did
mad

did
man

mat
Sid

Read the words. Circle the word that names the picture.
Then write the word.

Say the name of the pictures. Draw a line from each picture whose name begins with the same sound as *cap* to the cap.

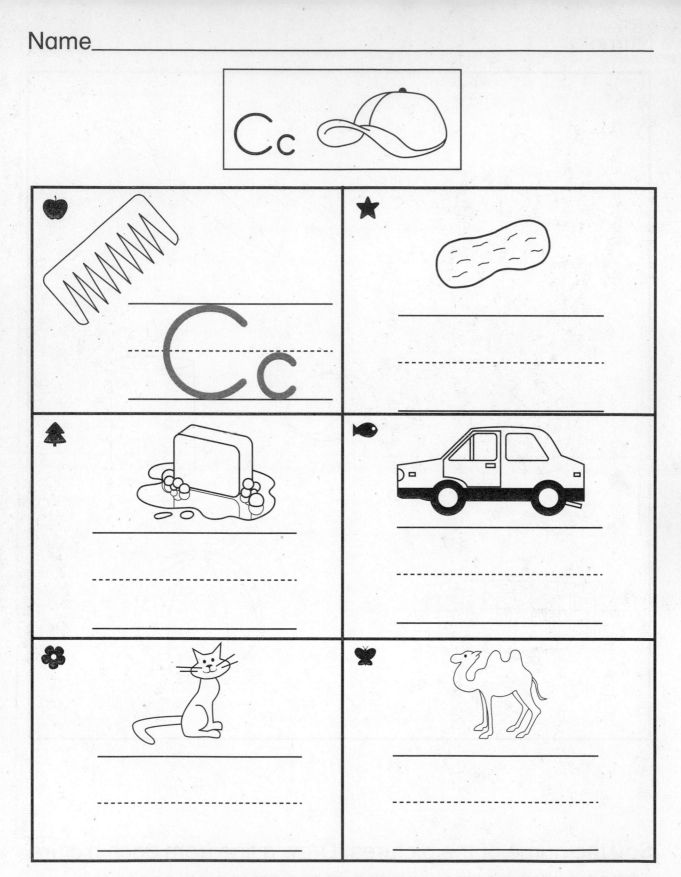

Say the name of each picture. If the name begins with the same sound as *cap*, write *Cc* on the line.

Say each picture name. Color the pictures in each row whose names begin with the same sound as *cap*.

Write *Cc* on the lines. Then say the names of the pictures. Circle each picture whose name begins with *Cc*.

C

c

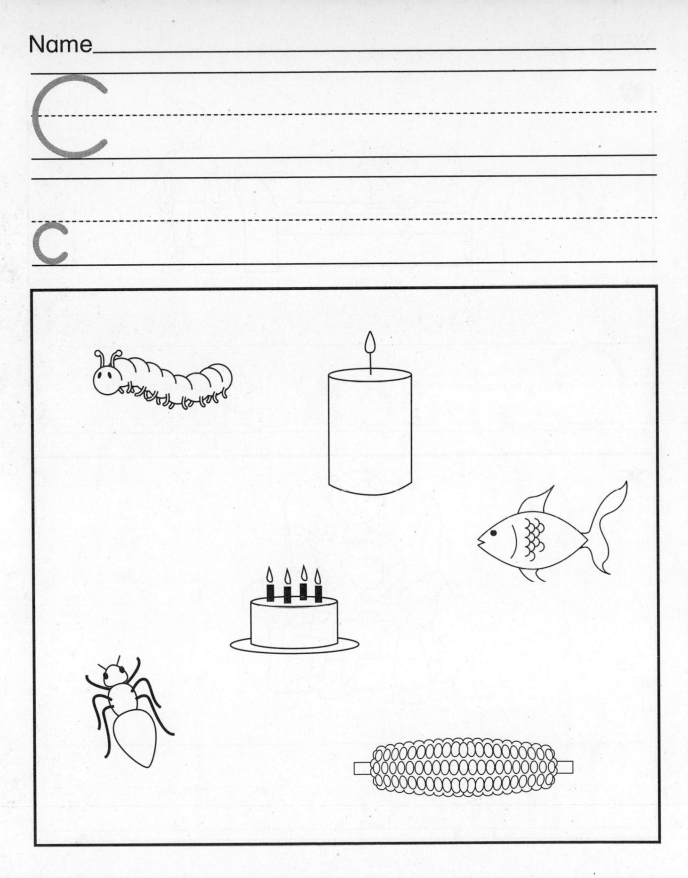

Trace and write *Cc*. Color the pictures whose names begin with the same sound as *cap*.

Name_____

Cat can sit.

Tim can sit.

Trace the words. Read the sentences. Where does Cat like to sit in each picture? Circle that part of the picture.

Name_____

Help the ostrich get to the octopus. Say the names of the pictures. Color the pictures that begin with the same sound as *ostrich.* Then draw a line to show the path.

Write *Oo* on the lines. Then say the names of the pictures.
Circle each picture whose name begins like *octopus*.

Say the name of the pictures. Draw a line from each picture whose name has the same middle sound as *pot* to the picture of the pot.

Say the picture name. Write the missing letter in each word.

Trace and write *Oo.* Then color the pictures that begin with the same sound as *ostrich.*

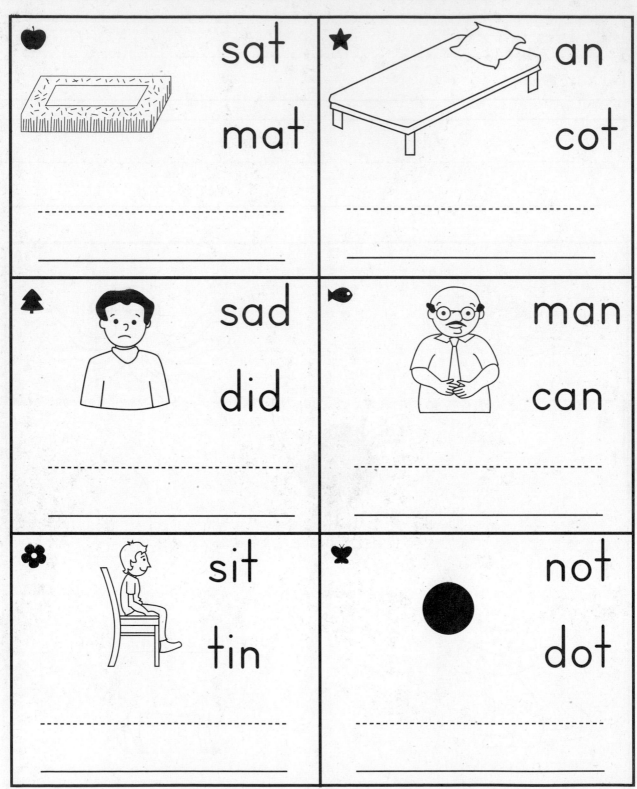

sat

mat

an

cot

sad

did

man

can

sit

tin

not

dot

Read the words. Circle the word that names the picture.
Then write the word.

Name_____

Say each picture name. Color the pictures in each row whose names begin with the same sound as *fish*.

F f

5

Ff

Say the name of each picture. If the name begins with the same sound as *fish*, write *Ff* on the line.

Name_____

Say the picture names. Circle the pictures whose names begin with the same sound as *five*.

F f

Write *Ff* on the lines. Then say the names of the pictures. Circle each picture whose name begins like *fish*.

Name_____

F
F

f
f

Trace and write *Ff.* Color the pictures whose names begin with the same sound as *fish.*

Tim is on it.

Mom is on it.

Tam is on it.

Trace the words. Read the sentences. What are Tim, Mom and Tam on? Circle that part of each picture.

Say each picture name. Circle the letter that stands for the beginning sound.

a i o

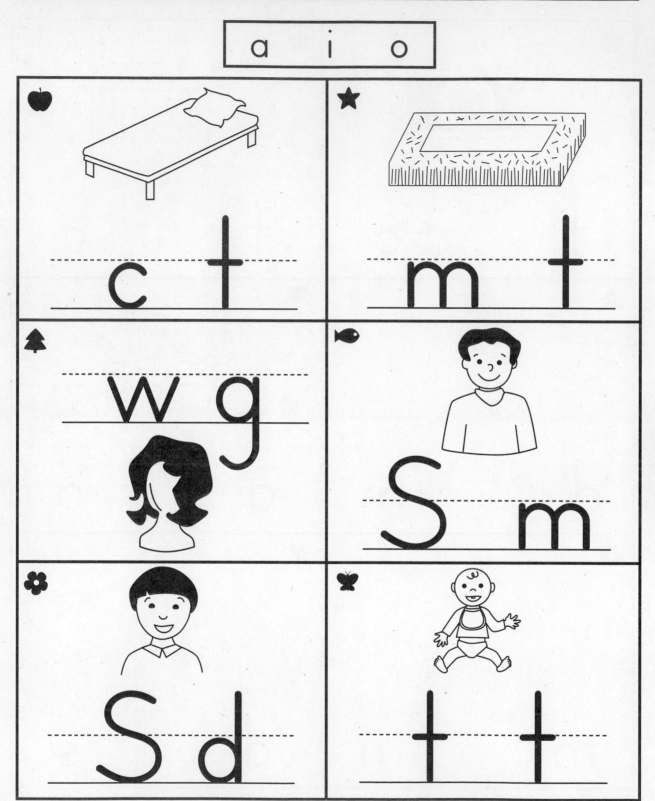

c t

m t

w g

S m

S d

t t

Say each picture name. Choose a letter from the box that
stands for the middle sound. Write the letter on the line.

Are you fit?

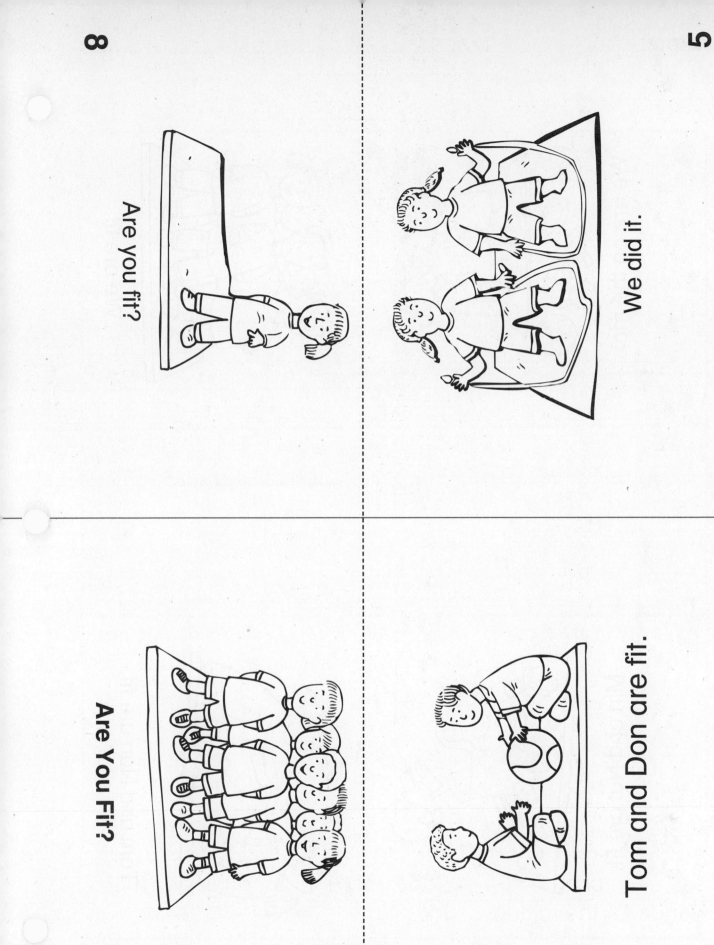

We did it.

Tom and Don are fit.

Are You Fit?

We are on the mat.

We are fit.

Are You Fit? McGraw-Hill School Division

Min and Nat are fit.

Tam and Nan are fit.

Name_____

Say the name of the pictures. Draw a line from each picture whose name begins like *robot* to the picture of the robot.

 Grade K

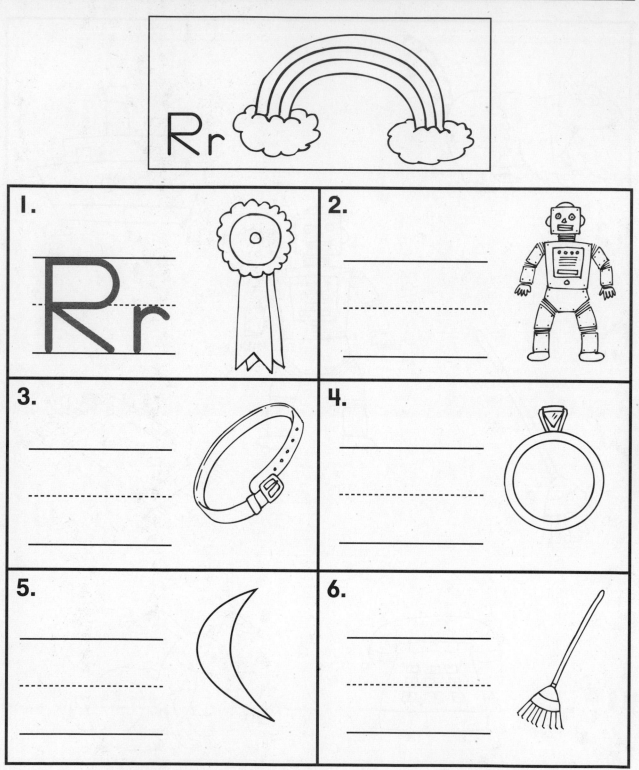

Say the name of each picture. If the name begins with the same sound as *rainbow,* write *Rr* on the line.

Look at the picture. Color the things whose names begin with the same sound as *rainbow*.

6 Grade K

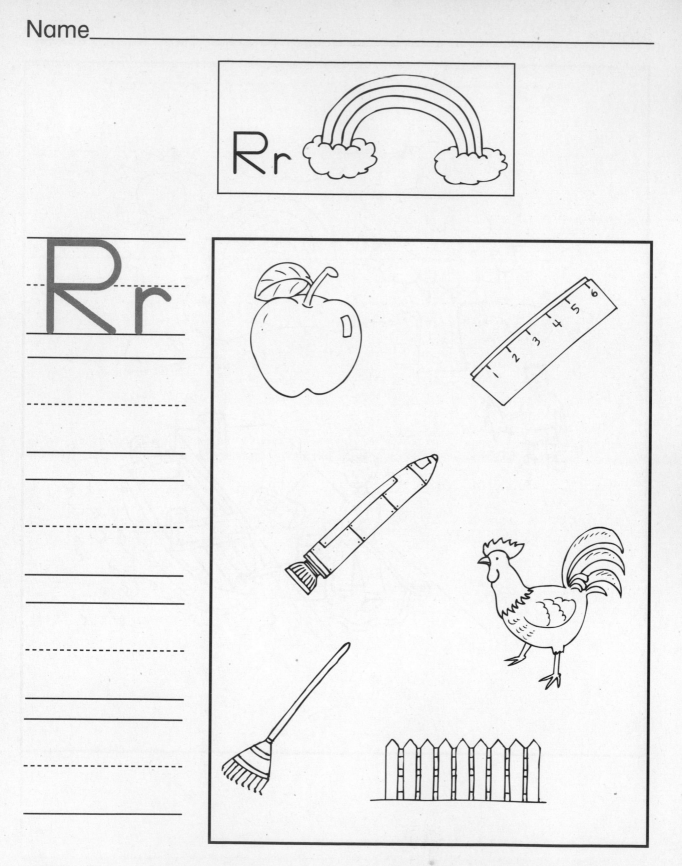

Rr

Write *Rr* on the lines. Say the names of the pictures. Circle each picture whose name begins the same as *rainbow*.

R

r

Trace and write *Rr.* Color the pictures whose names begin with the same sound as *rainbow.*

1. cat
   can
   _____

2. cot
   dot
   _____

3. fan
   fin
   _____

4. tot
   not
   _____

5. sat
   mat
   _____

6. man
   sad
   _____

Read the words. Then circle the word that names the picture. Write the word.

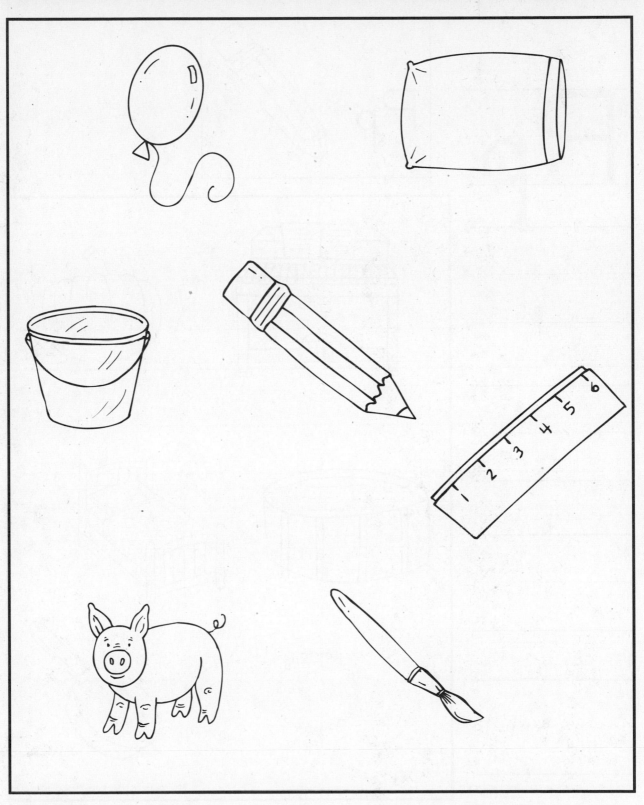

Say the names of the pictures. Draw a line from each picture whose name begins like *pencil* to the picture of the pencil.

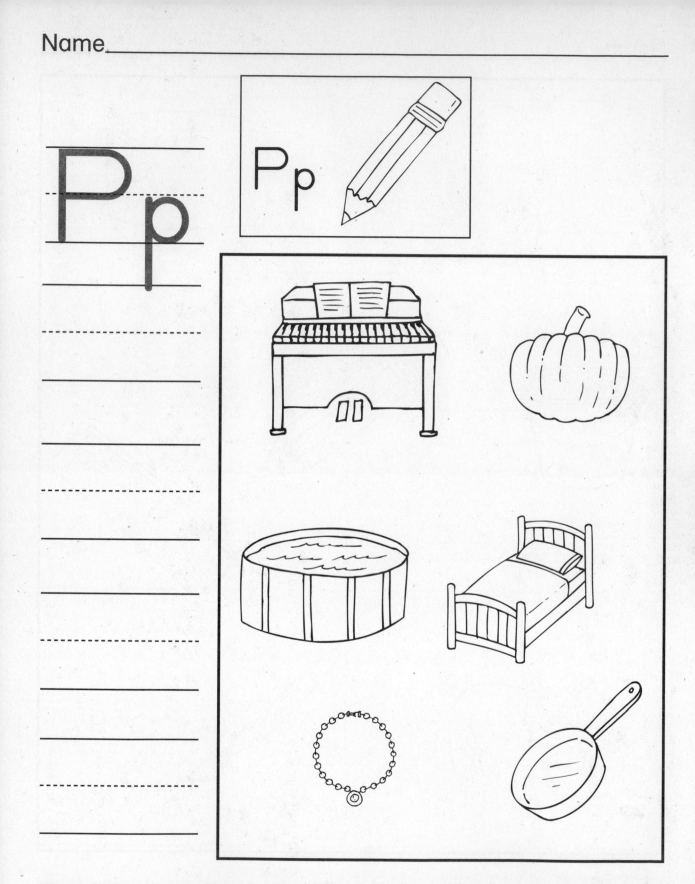

P p

Write _Pp_ on the lines. Say the names of the pictures. Circle each picture whose name begins the same as _pencil_.

Name_____

Say the picture names. Circle the pictures whose names end with the same sound as in *map*.

Grade K

1. p

2.

3.

4.

5.

6.

Say the name of each picture. If the picture name ends with the same sound as *map,* write *p* on the line.

P

P

p

p

Trace and write *Pp*. Then color the pictures whose names begin with the same sound as *pencil*.

Grade K

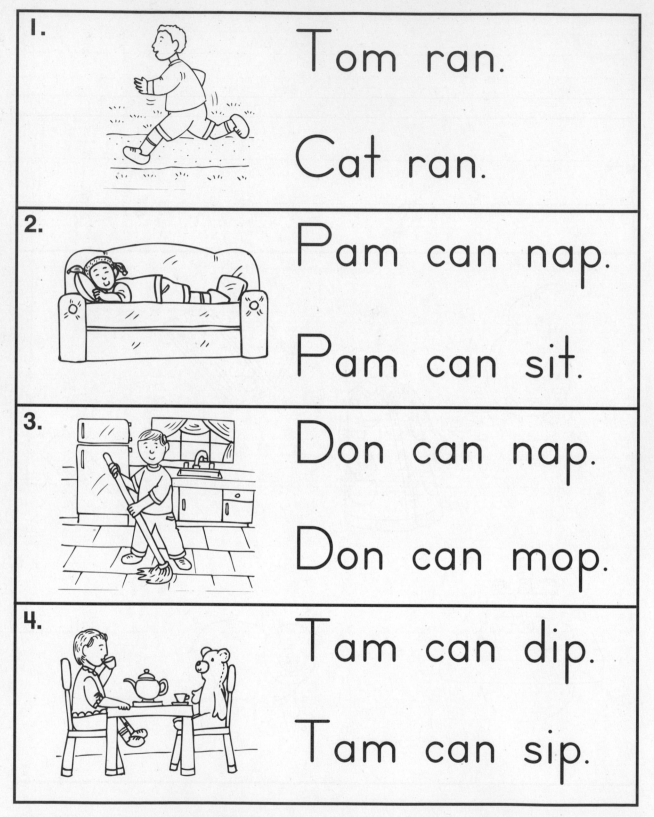

1. Tom ran.

   Cat ran.

2. Pam can nap.

   Pam can sit.

3. Don can nap.

   Don can mop.

4. Tam can dip.

   Tam can sip.

Look at the picture. Read the words. Circle the words that tell about the picture.

Name_____

Look at the picture. Color the things whose names begin with the same sound as *lion.*

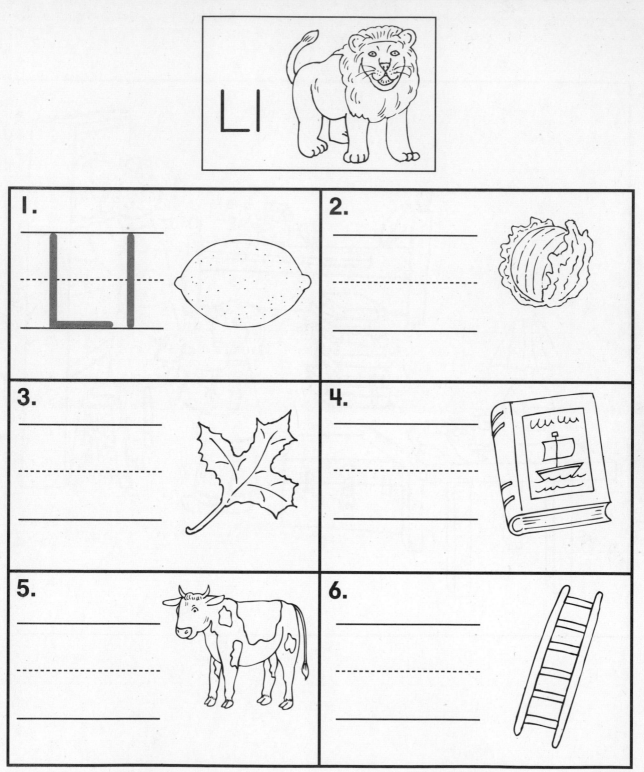

Ll

1. **Ll**

2.

3.

4.

5.

6.

Say the name of each picture. If the name begins with the same sound as *lion,* write *Ll* on the line.

Say the name of the pictures. Draw a line from each picture whose name begins with the same sound as *lion* to the picture of the lion.

Write *Ll* on the lines. Say the names of the pictures. Circle each picture whose name begins the same as *lion*.

Trace and write *Ll.* Then circle the pictures whose names begin with the same sound as *lion.*

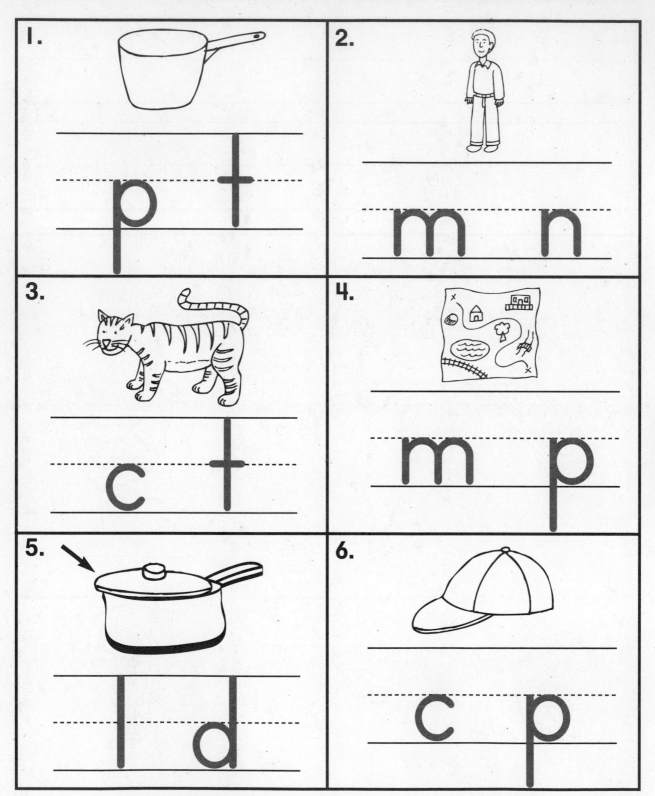

1. p t

2. m n

3. c t

4. m p

5. l d

6. c p

Name each picture. Trace the letters and write the letter for the missing middle sound. Then read the word.

McGraw-Hill School Division

1.

2.

3.

4.

Say each picture name. Circle the picture in each row whose name begins with the same sound as *uncle*.

Uu

Write *Uu* on the lines. Then say the name of the pictures.
Circle each picture whose name begins with the same
sound as *uncle*.

Say the names of the pictures. Draw a line from each picture whose name has the same middle sound as *bug* to the picture of the bug.

Grade K

__ u __

1.

2.

3.

4.

5.

6.

Say the name of each picture. If the name has the same middle sound as *sun*, write *u* on the line.

Name_____

U

u

Trace and write *Uu*. Then color the pictures whose names begin with the same sound as *umbrella*.

1.

Mom can run.

2.

Sid can run.

3.

Trace the words. Read the sentences. Then look at the bottom picture. Who else can run? Write a sentence.

Name_____

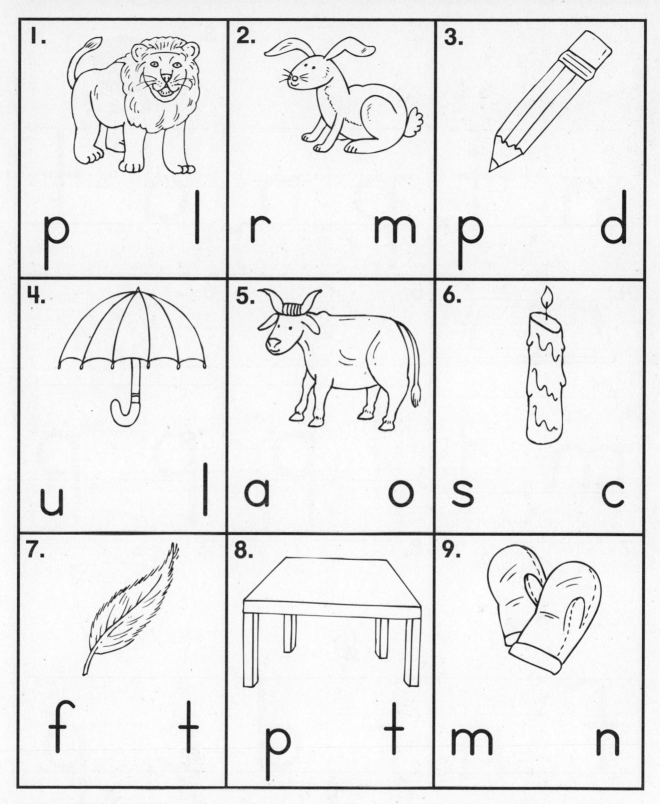

Say each picture name. Circle the letter that stands for the beginning sound.

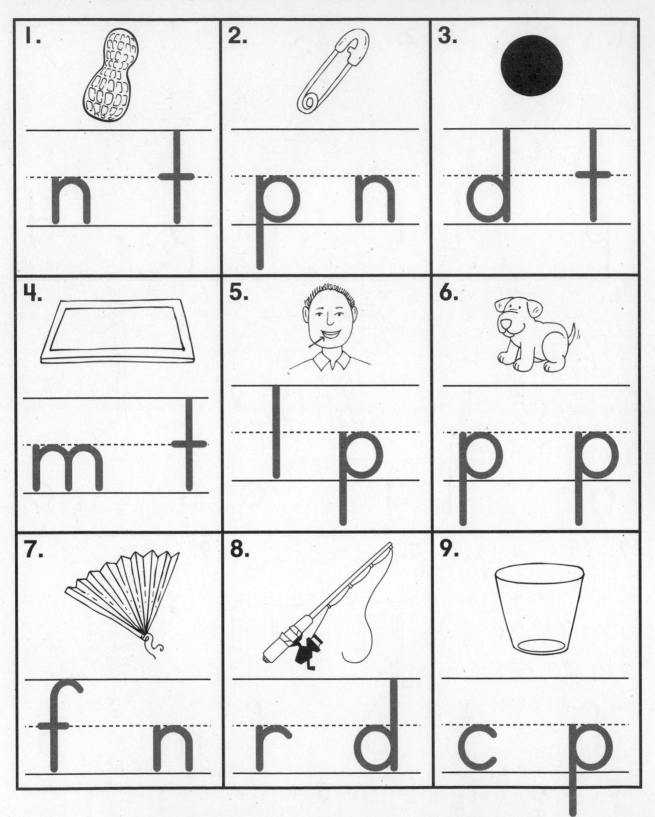

1. n t

2. p n

3. d t

4. m t

5. l p

6. p p

7. f n

8. r d

9. c p

Name each picture. Trace the letters and write the letters for the missing middle sound. Then read the word.

That mop top is my pup.

Is that mop top on the mat?

Mop Top and Me

Is that mop top on my cap?

Is mop top my pup?

Mop Top and Me McGraw-Hill School Division

Is that mop top on the cot?

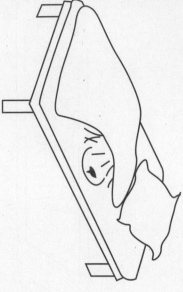

See that mop top go.

Is that mop top in the mud?

1.

2.

3.

4.

Say each picture name. Color the pictures in each row whose names begin with the same sound as *kite*.

K k

Write *Kk* on the lines. Say the names of the pictures. Color each picture whose name begins the same as *kite*.

Name_____

1.

2.

3.

4.

5.

6.

Say the picture names. Color the pictures whose names
end with the same sound as *lock*.

__ck

1.

ck

2.

3.

4.

5.

6.

Say the name of each picture. If the name has the same ending sound as *lock,* write *ck* on the line.

Grade K   6

K

k

Trace and write *Kk*. Color the pictures whose names begin with the same sound as *kite*.

8 Grade K

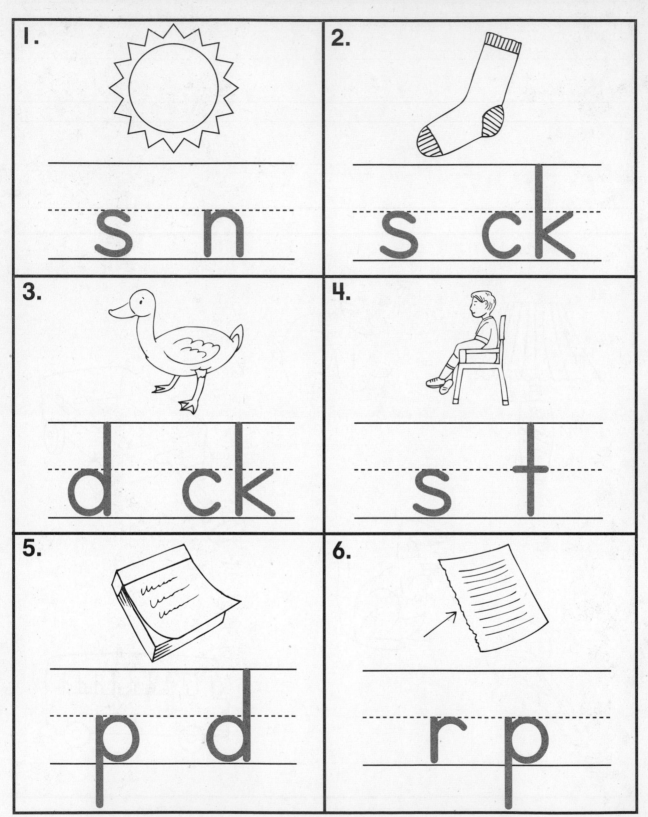

1. s __ n

2. s __ ck

3. d __ ck

4. s __ t

5. p __ d

6. r __ p

Name each picture. Trace the letters and write the letter for the missing middle sound. Then read the word.

Say the names of the pictures. Draw a line from each picture whose name begins with the same sound as *gate* to the picture of the gate.

Gg

1.

2.

3.

Gg

4.

5.

6.

Say the name of each picture. If the name begins with the same sound as *gift,* write *Gg* on the line.

Name_____

Say each picture name. Color the pictures in each row whose names end with the same sound as *frog*.

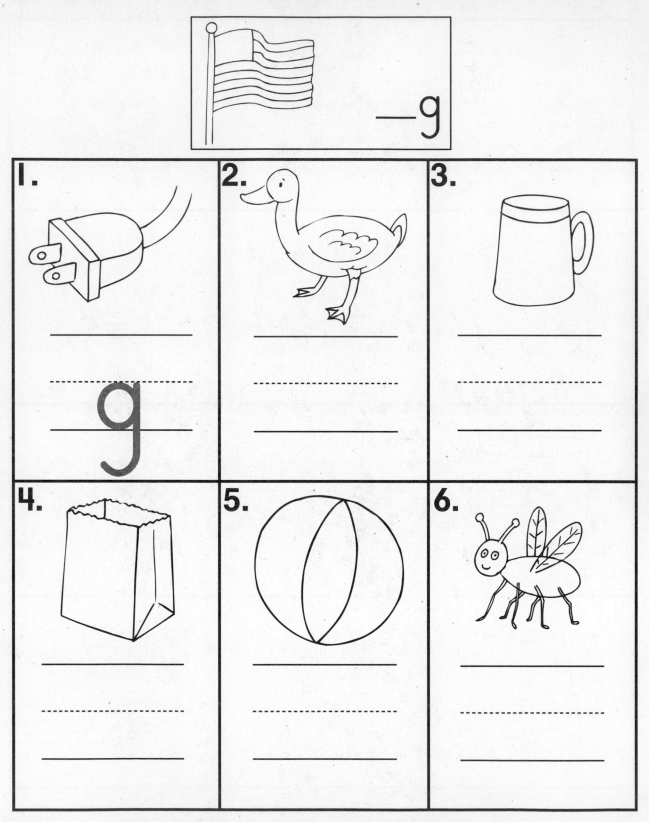

Say the name of each picture. If the picture name ends with the same sound as *flag*, write *g* on the line.

G

g

Trace and write *Gg*. Circle the pictures whose names begin with the same sound as *gate*.

Grade K

1.

pup   cup

bug on

2.

sock   rock

bug on

3.

lip   lid

bug on

4.

cap   lad

bug on

Look at each picture. Where is the bug? Circle the word that tells where the bug is. Then write the word.

Say the names of the pictures. Color the pictures that begin with the same sound as *eggs.*

Grade K

E e

Write *Ee* on the lines. Say the names of the pictures. Circle each picture whose name begins the same as *egg*.

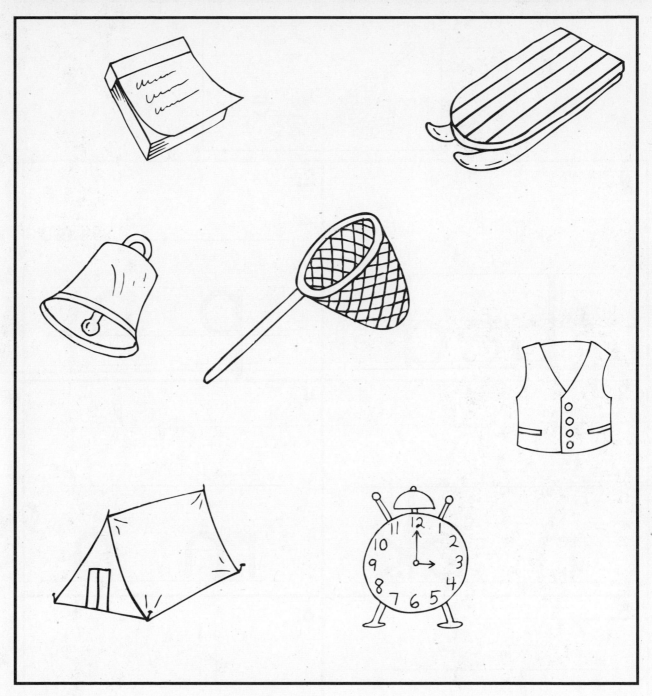

Say the names of the pictures. Draw a line from each picture whose name has the same middle sound as in *net* to the picture of the net.

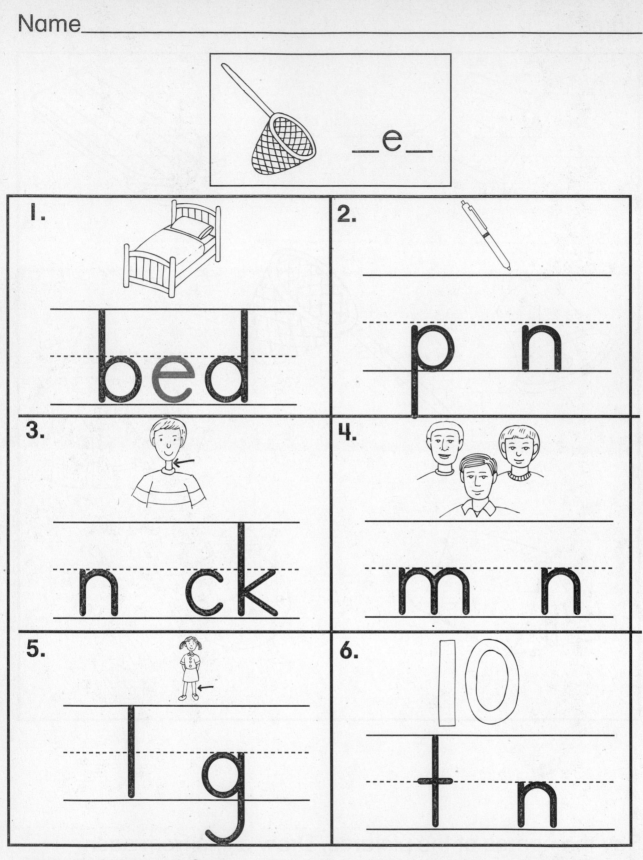

_e_

1. b e d

2. p _ n

3. n _ c k

4. m _ n

5. l _ g

6. t _ n

Say the picture name. Write the missing letter in each word.

E

e

Trace and write *Ee*. Color the pictures whose names begin with the same sound as *egg*.

1. kick rock

2. mug rug

3. tack sack

4. bag rag

5. dad sad

6. bed red

Read the words. Circle the word that names the picture. Then write the word.

1.

2.

3.

4.

Say each picture name. Circle the pictures in each row whose names begin with the same sound as *book*.

Say the name of each picture. If the name begins with the same sound as *book,* write *Bb* on the line.

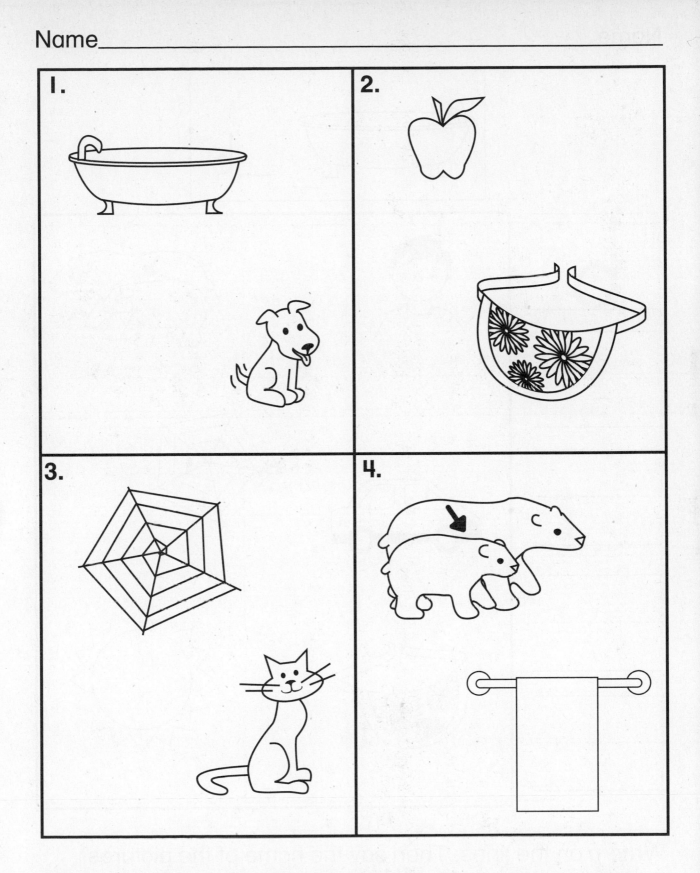

1.

2.

3.

4.

Say each picture name. Circle the pictures whose names end with the same sound as *rub*.

Write *b* on the lines. Then say the name of the pictures.
Circle the pictures whose names end with the same sound
as *tub.*

Name_____

B

b

Trace and write *Bb*. Color the pictures that have the same beginning sound as *book*.

Grade K

1.

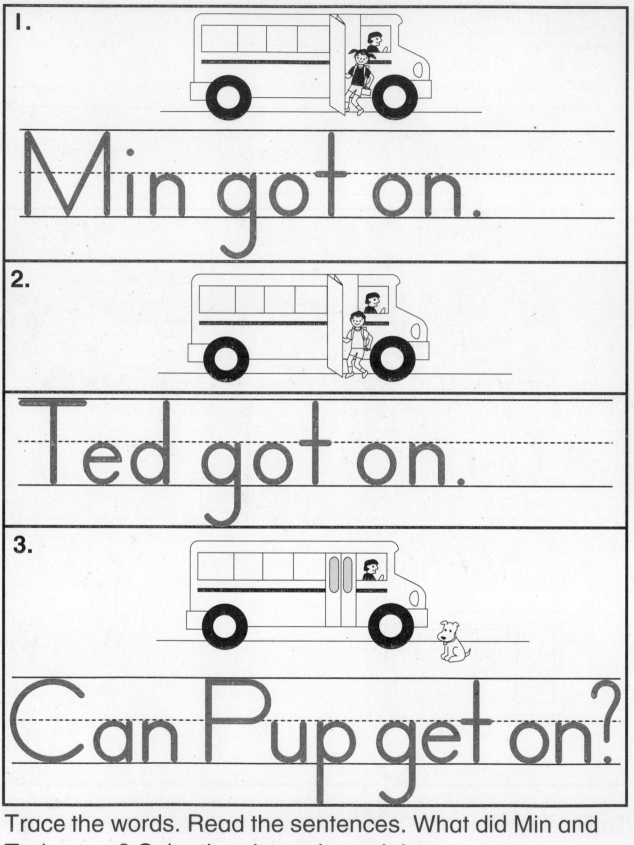

Min got on.

2.

Ted got on.

3.

Can Pup get on?

Trace the words. Read the sentences. What did Min and Ted get on? Color the picture in each box.

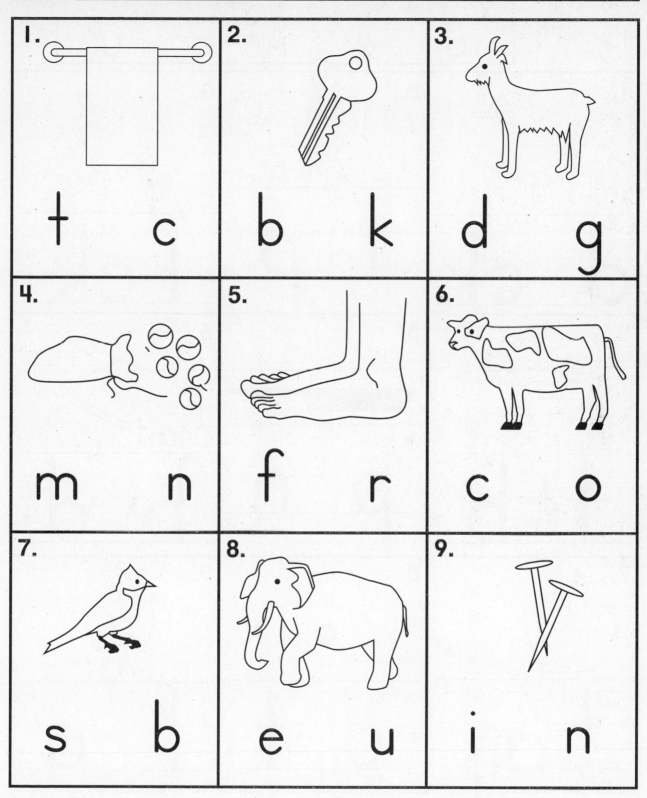

1. t c

2. b k

3. d g

4. m n

5. f r

6. c o

7. s b

8. e u

9. i n

Say each picture name. Circle the letter that stands for the beginning sound.

9 Grade K

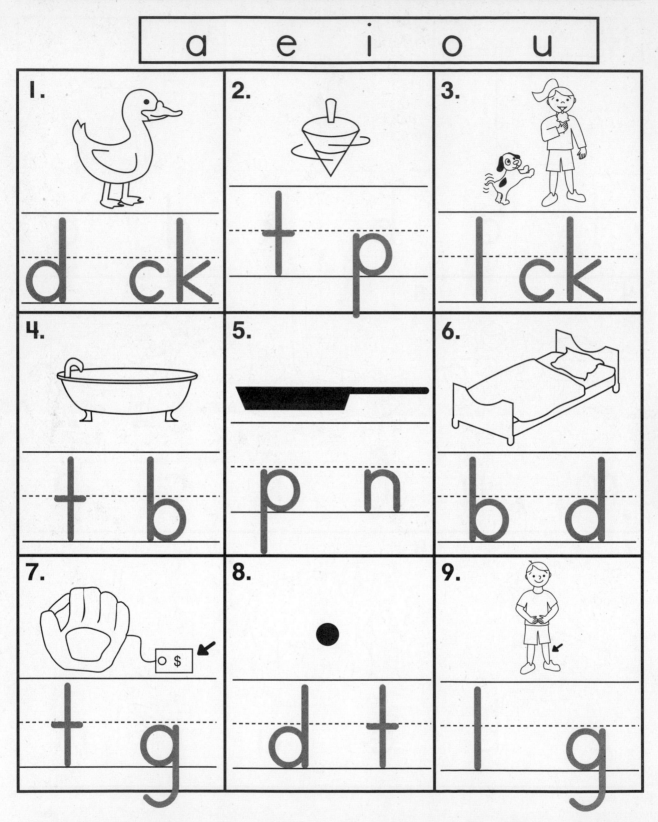

| a | e | i | o | u |

1. d __ ck

2. t __ p

3. l __ ck

4. t __ b

5. p __ n

6. b __ d

7. t __ g

8. d __ t

9. l __ g

Trace the letters. Choose a letter from the box that stands for the middle sound. Write the letter. Then read the word.

Grade K 9

Mick and Mack have Pug.

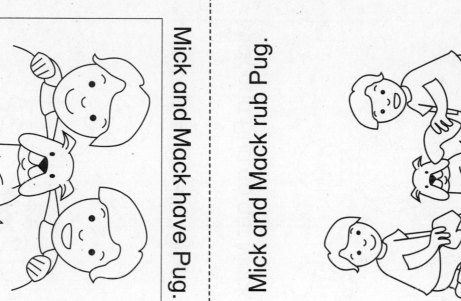

Mick and Mack rub Pug.

Pug, the Pet

Pug is in the tub.

Mick and Pug go get Mack.

Pug can tug at Mack.

"He is **MY** pet," said Mick.

"Pug is **MY** pet," said Mack.

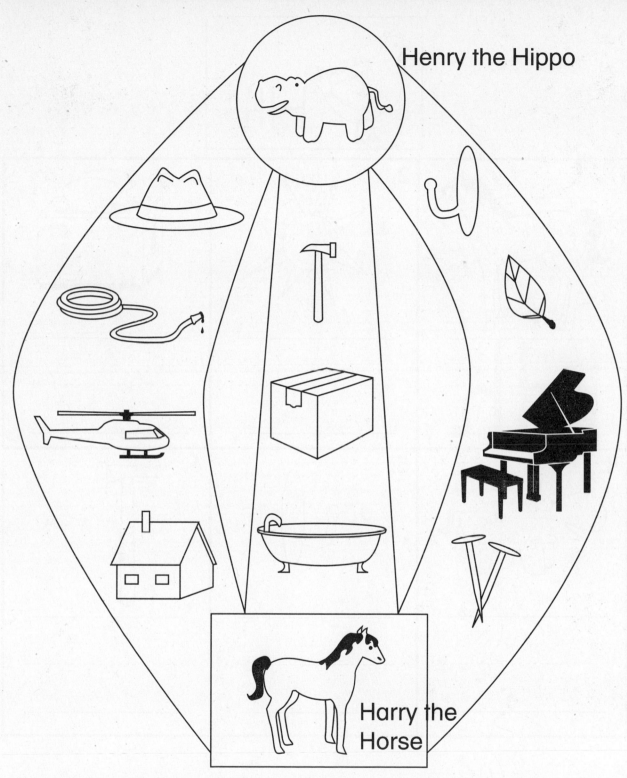

Henry the Hippo

Harry the Horse

Help the Hippo get to the Horse. Say the name of each picture. Draw a line on the path that only shows pictures whose names begin with the same sound as *hen*.

Name_____

1. **2.** **3.**

Hh

4. **5.** **6.**

Say the name of each picture. If the name begins with the same sound as *hen,* write *Hh* on the line.

Say the names of the pictures. Draw a line from each picture whose name begins with the same sound as *house* to the picture of the house.

Write *Hh* on the lines. Then say the names of the pictures.
Color each picture whose name begins with the same
sound as *hen*.

H

h

Trace and write *Hh.* Then circle the pictures that have the same beginning sound as *hen.*

Name_____

| a | e | i | o | u |

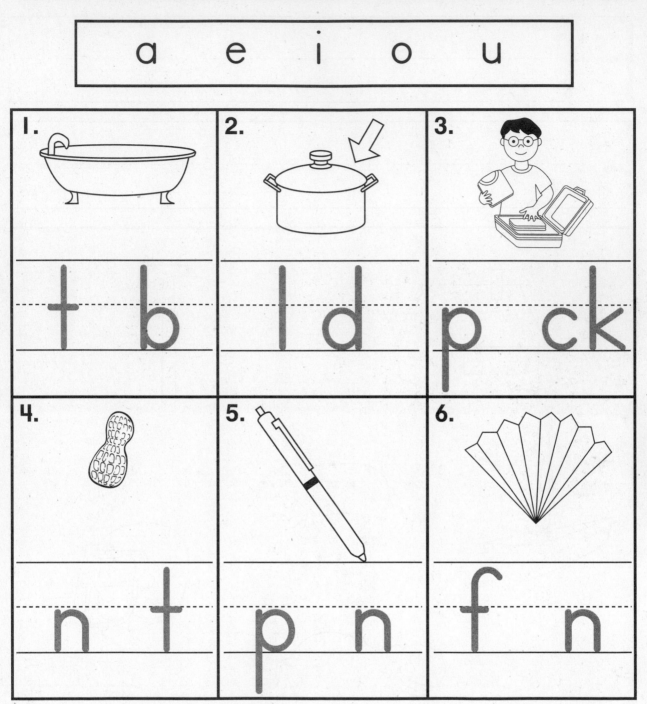

1.	2.	3.
t b	l d	p __ ck
4.	5.	6.
n t	p n	f n

Trace the letters in each picture name. Choose a letter
from the box that stands for the middle sound. Write the
letter on the line. Then read the word.

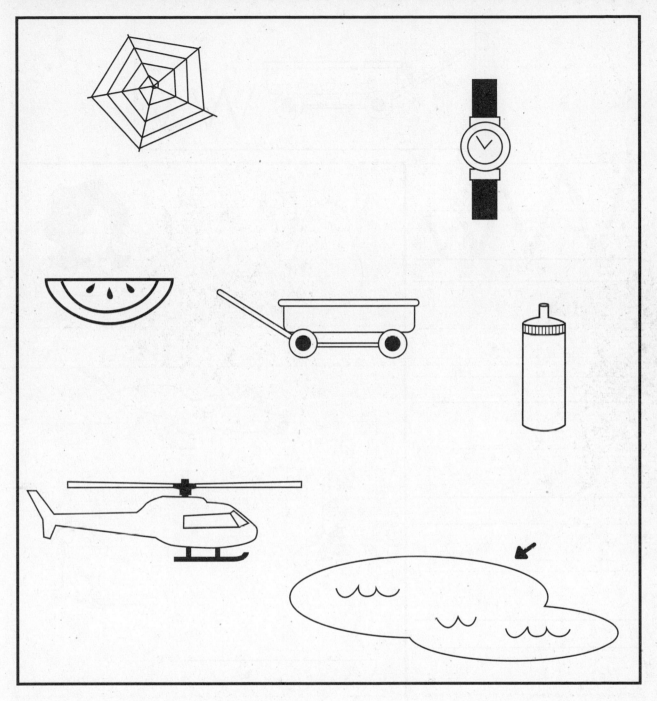

Say the names of the pictures. Draw a line from each picture whose name begins with the same sound as *wagon* to the picture of the wagon.

Grade K

Write *Ww* on the lines. Then say the names of the pictures.
Circle each picture that begins with the same sound as
wagon.

Look at the picture. Color the things whose names begin with the same sound as *wet*.

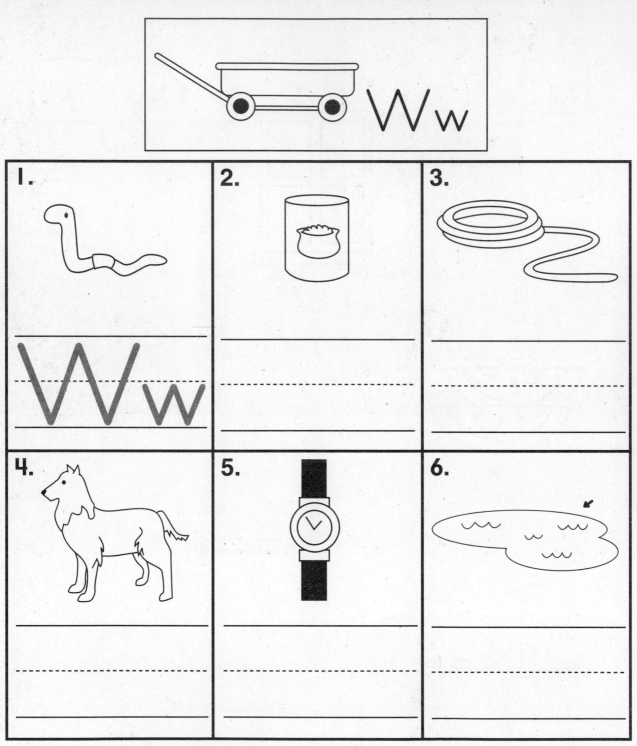

Say the name of each picture. If the name begins with the same sound as *wagon,* write *Ww* on the line.

W

w

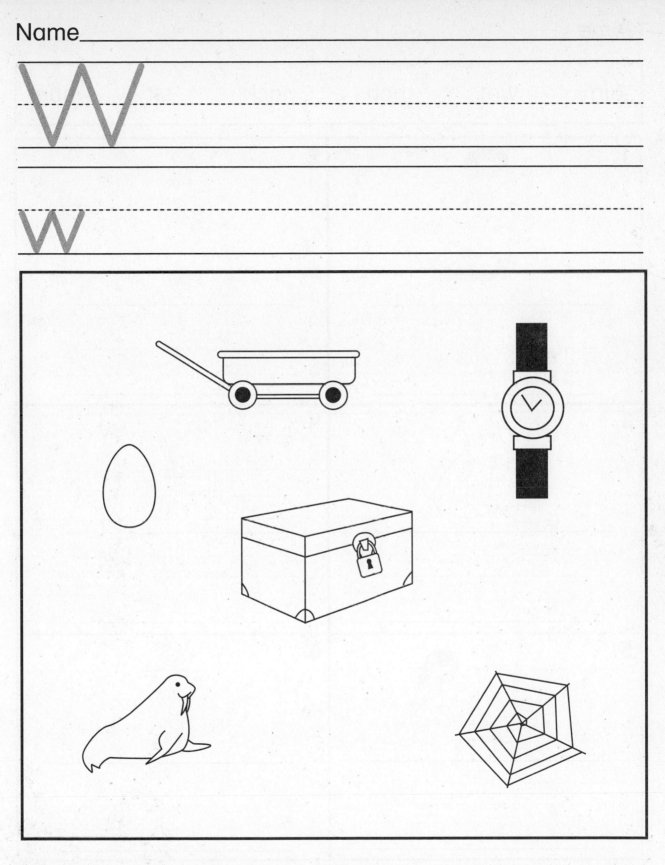

Trace and write *Ww.* Then circle the pictures whose names begin with the same sound as *wagon.*

| dig | wet | hop | pack | sit | hug |

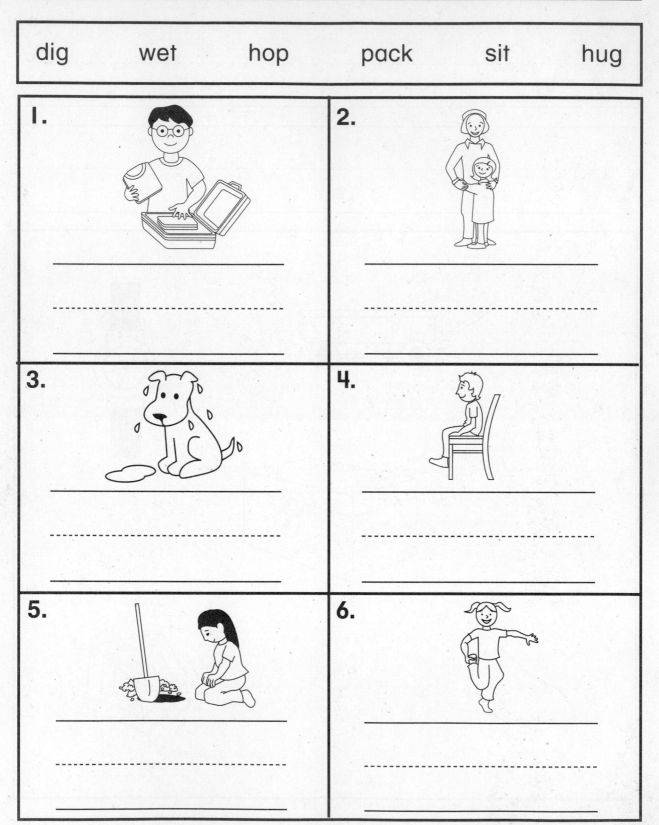

1.

_____

- -

_____

2.

_____

- -

_____

3.

_____

- -

_____

4.

_____

- -

_____

5.

_____

- -

_____

6.

_____

- -

_____

Read the words. Write the word that tells about each picture.

Say the names of the pictures. Draw a line from each picture whose name begins like *vest* to the picture of the vest.

6

Say the name of each picture. If the name begins with the same sound as *vest*, write *Vv* on the line.

Name_____

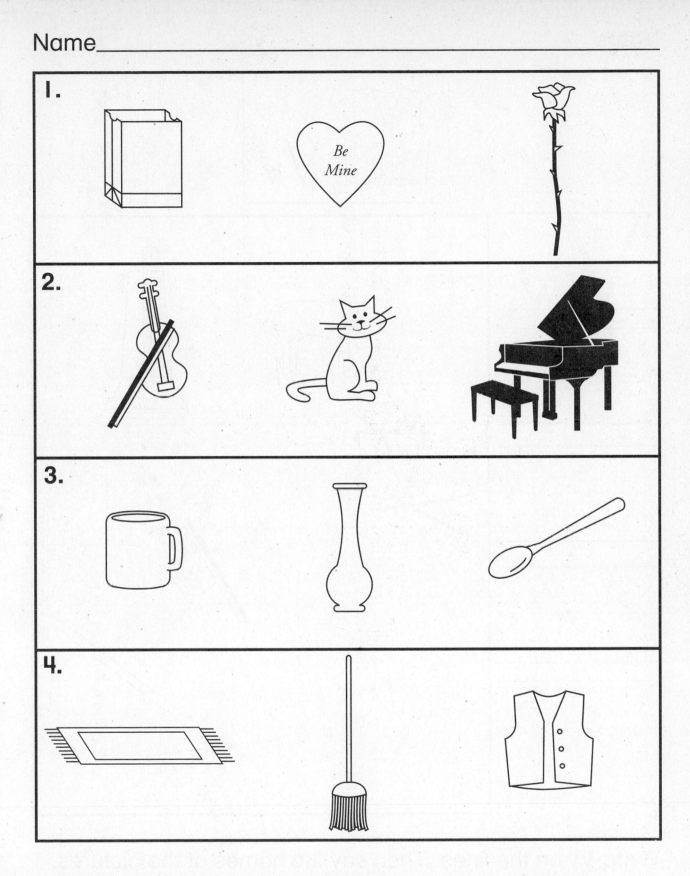

1.

2.

3.

4.

Say each picture name. Circle the picture in each row whose name begins with the same sound as *van*.

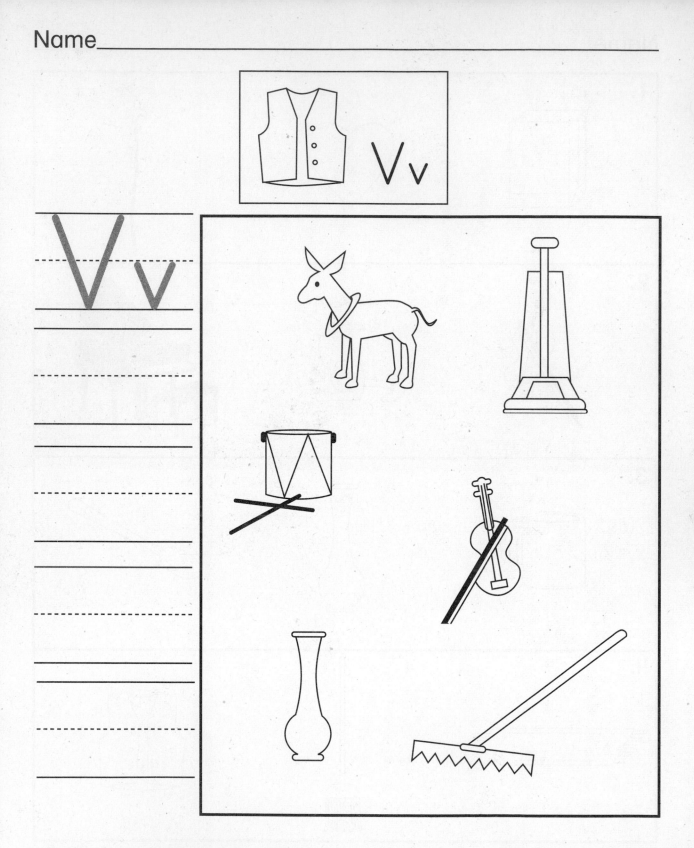

Write *Vv* on the lines. Then say the names of the pictures.
Circle each picture whose name begins with the same
sound as *vest*.

Name_____

V

V

Trace and write *Vv*. Color the pictures whose names begin with the same sound as *vest*.

1.

Pam can _____.

pack   pick

2.

Don can _____.

run   red

3.

Min can _____.

dig   dot

4.

Ben can _____.

top   tag

Look at the picture. Circle the correct word to finish the sentence. Then write the word on the line.

Say the names of the pictures. Draw a line from each picture whose name ends with the same sound as *box* to the box.

Grade K

Write *x* on the lines. Then say the names of the pictures.
Color each picture that has the same ending sound as *box*.

Name_____

1.

2.

3.

6   **10**

4.

5.

6.

Say the picture names. Circle the pictures that have the
same ending sound as *fix*.

1.

6

x

2.

3.

4.

5.

6.

Say the name of each picture. Write *x* on the line if the picture name ends with the same sound as *box*.

Trace *Xx*. Then circle the pictures that have the same ending sound as *box*.

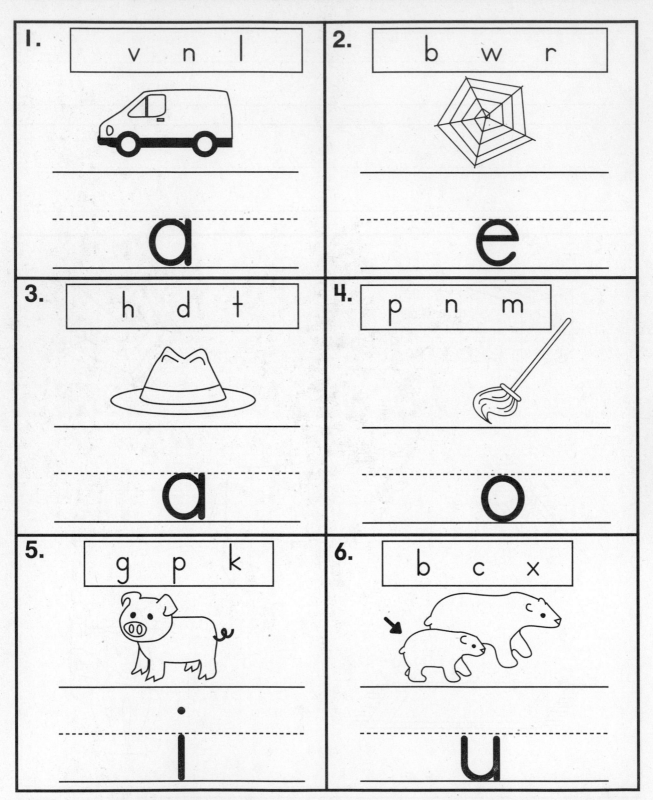

1.

| v | n | l |

a

2.

| b | w | r |

e

3.

| h | d | t |

a

4.

| p | n | m |

o

5.

| g | p | k |

i

6.

| b | c | x |

u

Name each picture. Choose the letters you need from the box to make the picture name. Write the letters.

Color the things whose names begin with the same sound as *quilt*.

Grade K

1. ?

qu

2.

3.

4.

5.

6.

Say the name of each picture. Write *qu* on the line if the name begins with the same sound as *quilt*.

1.

2.

3.

4.

Say each picture name. Circle the picture in each row
whose name begins with the same sound as *quick.*

Grade K

qu

Write *qu* on the lines. Then say the names of the pictures.
Circle each picture whose name begins with the same
sound as *quilt*.

Qu

qu

Trace and write *Qu, qu.* Then circle the pictures whose names begin with the same sound as *quick.*

8 Grade K

1. Rex can _____ it.

wax   fix

2. Meg can _____ .

hop   hit

3. Ned can _____ .

cut   cat

4. Tam can _____ .

pet   pack

Look at the picture. Circle the correct word to finish the sentence. Then write the word on the line.

1.

2.

3.

4.

Say each picture name. Circle the pictures in each row
whose names begin with the same sound as *jam.*

J j

J j

Write *Jj* on the lines. Then say the names of the pictures.
Circle each picture whose name begins with the same
sound as *jar*.

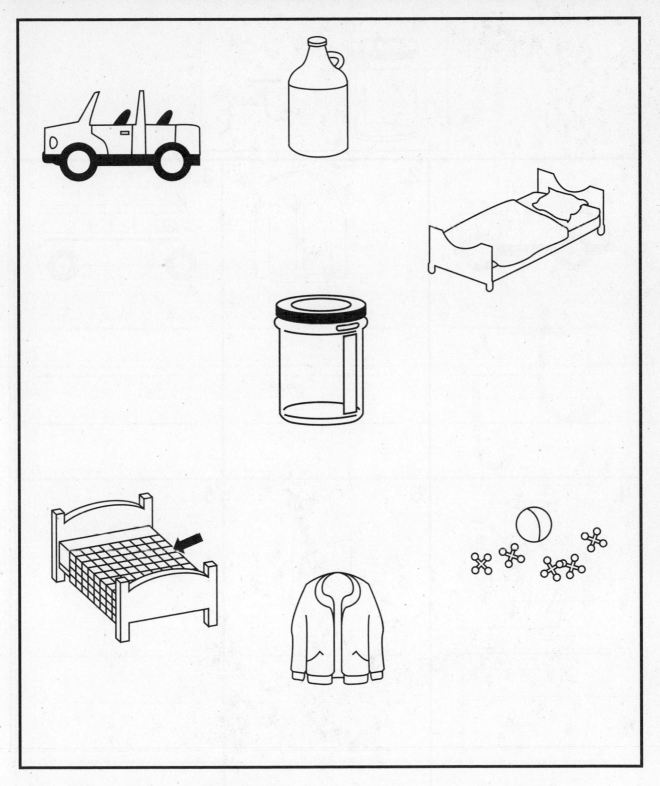

Say the names of the pictures. Draw a line from each picture whose name begins with the same sound as *jar* to the picture of the jar.

Grade K

Say the name of each picture. Write *Jj* on the line if the
name begins with the same sound as *jar*.

Name_____

J

J

j

j

Trace and write *Jj*. Then color the pictures whose names begin with the same sound as *jam*.

8 Grade K

jet	fox	vet
bag	bug	ham

1.

_____

- - - - - - - - - - -

_____

2.

_____

- - - - - - - - - - -

_____

3.

_____

- - - - - - - - - - -

_____

4.

_____

- - - - - - - - - - -

_____

Read the words in the box. Write the word that names each picture.

Say each picture name. Circle the picture in each row
whose name begins with the same sound as *yard*.

Write *Yy* on the lines. Then say the names of the pictures. Circle each picture whose name begins with the same sound as *yo-yo*.

1.

2.

3.

4.

5.

6.

Say the picture names. Circle the pictures whose names begin with the same sound as *yum.*

Say the name of each picture. Write *Yy* on the line if the name begins with the same sound as *yo-yo*.

Y

Y

y

Trace and write *Yy*. Color the pictures whose names begin with the same sound as *yo-yo*.

| a | e | i | o | u |

1. m t

2. l ck

3. h n

4. 6 s x

Look at the letters in the box. Then name each picture. Trace the letters and write the missing letter. Read the word.

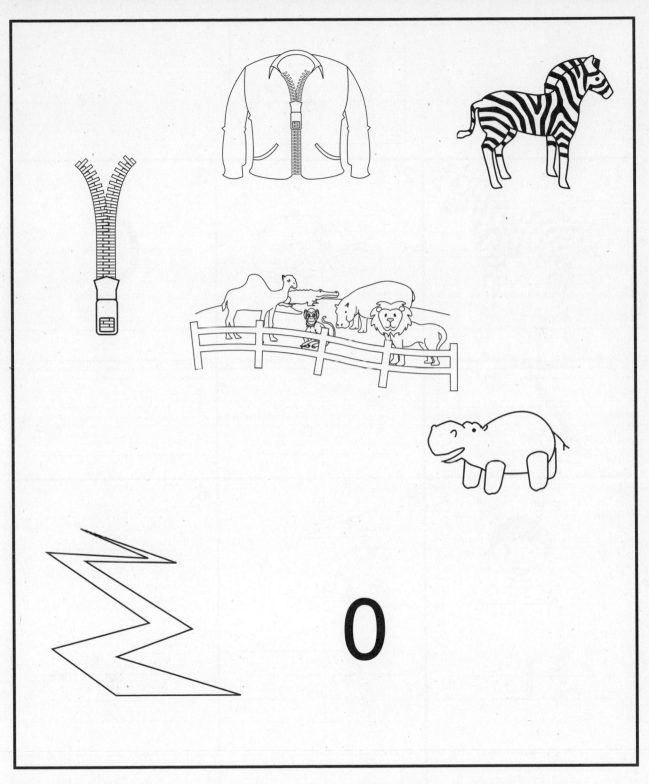

Say the names of the pictures. Draw a line from each picture whose name begins with the same sound as *zoo* to the picture of the zoo.

Zz

1.

2.

3.

0

Zz

4.

5.

6.

Say the name of each picture. Write *Zz* on the line if the
name begins with the same sound as *zipper*.

1.

2. 6   10   0

3.

4.

Say each picture name. Circle the picture in each row whose name begins with the same sound as *zip.*

Grade K

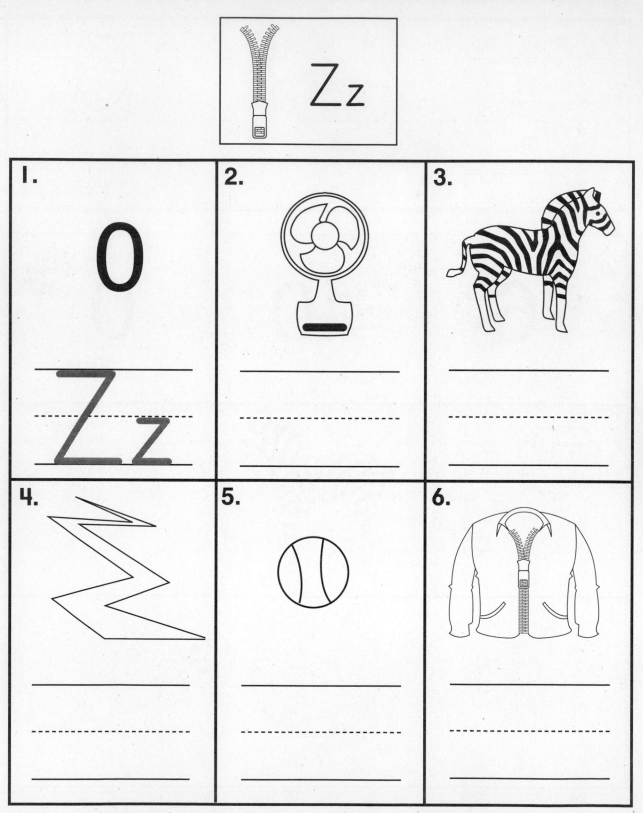

Zz

1.

O

Zz

2.

3.

4.

5.

6.

Say the name of each picture. Write *Zz* on the line if the name begins with the same sound as *zipper*.

Grade K 6

Z

z

Trace and write *Zz.* Color the pictures whose names begin with the same sound as *zipper.*

Grade K

1. Max can _____.

job   jog

2. Ken let Rex _____.

run   rip

3. Jen can _____.

men   mix

4. Min can _____.

wax   win

Look at each picture. Then read the sentence. Circle the word that completes each sentence. Write the word.

McGraw-Hill School Division

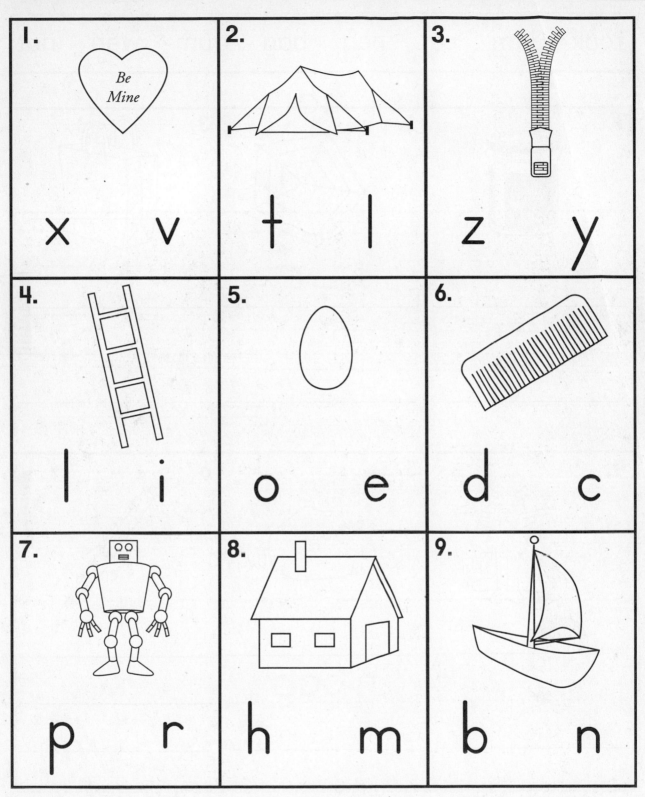

1.	2.	3.
x v	t l	z y
4.	**5.**	**6.**
l i	o e	d c
7.	**8.**	**9.**
p r	h m	b n

Say each picture name. Circle the letter that stands for the beginning sound of each picture name.

| rock | jam | cat | pen | bag | gum | web | nut |

1.

2.

3.

4.

5.

6.

Read the words in the box. Then look at each picture. Write a word from the box to name each picture.

Ned was quick to go to bed!

Can I have a sip?

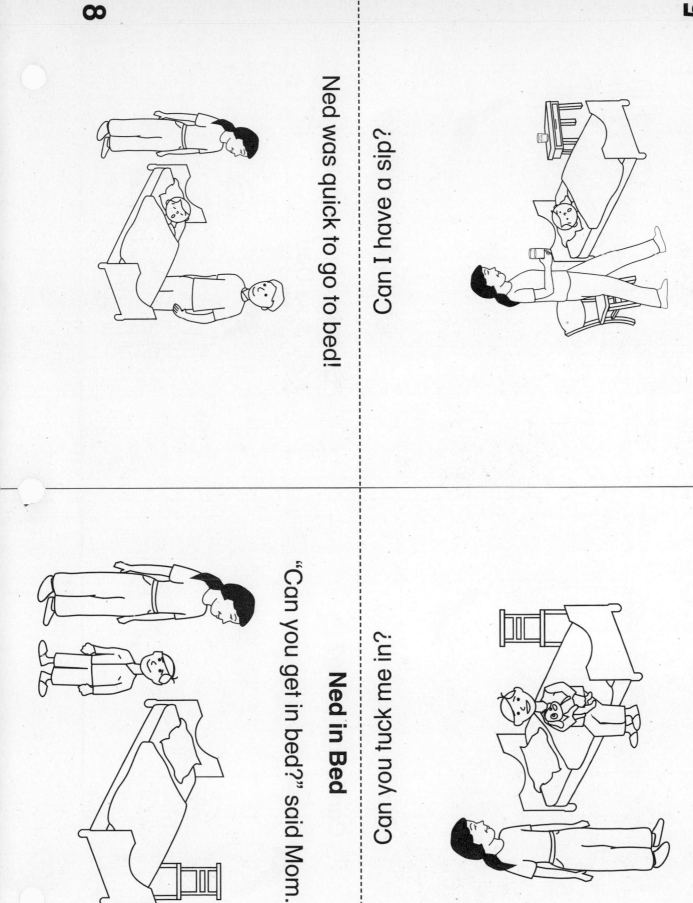

Ned in Bed

Can you tuck me in?

"Can you get in bed?" said Mom.

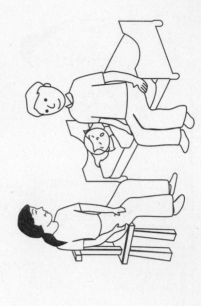

"Go to bed and we will sit with you," said Dad.

Can you hum to me?

Can I have a hug?

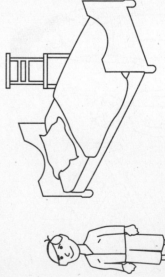

Can I have my pup?